Hume
on knowledge

'This book is written with admirable clarity, contains concise and helpful historical background, examines all the major issues in Hume's epistemology including important sections of the *Treatise* which are all too often skipped over, and gives a good sense of scholarly controversies among commentators on the *Treatise*. It is an excellent introduction to Hume for both undergraduates and beginning graduate students, and contains material which should be of interest even to Hume scholars.'

Francis W. Dauer, University of California, Santa Barbara

'This book gives us an accessible and philosophically sound discussion of the main themes of Hume's *Treatise*.'

R.S. Woolhouse, University of York

David Hume (1711–76) is one of the greatest figures in the history of British philosophy. Of all of Hume's writings, the philosophically most profound is undoubtedly his first, *A Treatise of Human Nature*. Of the three books that make up the *Treatise*, the first, in which he outlines the epistemology and metaphysics underpinning his system, is universally acknowledged to be his greatest intellectual achievement.

Hume on Knowledge thus provides us with a map to Book 1 of the *Treatise* and sets out its principal ideas and arguments in a clear and readable way. This book will enable any reader coming to the *Treatise* for the first time easily to understand the importance of and intricacies inherent in Hume's thought.

Harold W. Noonan is a Reader in Philosophical Logic at the University of Birmingham. He is the author of *Objects and Identity* and *Personal Identity* (available from Routledge).

**Routledge
Philosophy
GuideBooks**

Edited by Tim Crane and Jonathan Wolff
University College London

Kant and the *Critique of Pure Reason*
Sebastian Gardner

Mill on Liberty
Jonathan Riley

Mill on Utilitarianism
Roger Crisp

Wittgenstein and the *Philosophical Investigations*
Marie McGinn

Heidegger and *Being and Time*
Stephen Mulhall

Plato and the *Republic*
Nickolas Pappas

Locke on Government
D.A. Lloyd Thomas

Locke on Human Understanding
E.J. Lowe

Spinoza and Ethics
Genevieve Lloyd

LONDON AND NEW YORK

Routledge Philosophy GuideBook to

Hume
on knowledge

■ Harold W. Noonan

First published 1999 by Routledge
11 New Fetter Lane,
London EC4P 4EE

Simultaneously published in the USA
and Canada
by Routledge
29 West 35th Street, New York, NY
10001

*Routledge is an imprint of the Taylor &
Francis Group*

© 1999 Harold W. Noonan

Typeset in Times by Routledge
Printed and bound in Great Britain by
Clays Ltd, St Ives plc

*British Library Cataloguing in
Publication Data*
A catalogue record for this book is
available from the British Library

*Library of Congress Cataloging in
Publication Data*
Noonan, Harold W.
  Routledge philosophy guidebook to
Hume on knowledge / Harold W.
Noonan.
    p. cm.
  Includes bibliographical references
and index.
1. Hume, David, 1711–1776.
Treatise of human nature.
  Book 1. 2. Knowledge, Theory of. 3.
  Philosophy of mind. I. Title.
B1489.N66 1999
128–dc21   99–14365

ISBN 0–415–15046–9 (hbk)
ISBN 0–415–15047–7 (pbk)

To the memory of Barrie Falk (1940–98)

Contents

Preface

In this book I present a study of the most important themes in Book 1 of Hume's first, and greatest, work: *A Treatise of Human Nature*. The exposition follows the order in which these themes appear in the *Treatise*. Thus, after an introductory chapter outlining the background to Hume's thought and relating Book 1 of the *Treatise* to the rest of his work, the second chapter examines Hume's theory of the mind, as found in Part I of Book 1; the third chapter is devoted to Hume's discussion of causation, induction and the idea of necessary connection in Part III; and the remaining two chapters are concerned with the most significant and influential of Hume's discussions in Part IV: Section 2, on belief in the external world, and Section 6, on personal identity.

I am grateful to my colleagues at the University of Birmingham for the patience with which they have read and commented on successive redraftings of this material.

References have been given in general according to the Harvard referencing system. However references to Locke's *An Essay Concerning Human Understanding* are by book, chapter and section. Other occasional exceptions to the Harvard system are explained in the bibliography.

H.W.N.

Chapter 1

Introduction

Hume's life and work

Hume's life and times

David Hume, the last of the so-called 'three great British empiricists' – the others being Locke (1632–1704) and Berkeley (1685–1753) – was born on 26 April 1711, in Edinburgh, seven years after the death of Locke and when Berkeley was a young man of 26. His father was Joseph Home of Ninewells, a small landholding in Berwick-on-Tweed (David adopted the spelling 'Hume' when he left Scotland in 1734 to avoid mispronunciation by the English). His family were quite prosperous gentry and strict Presbyterians.

Hume's father died when he was only two and his mother never remarried. He was a precocious reader, described by his mother as 'uncommonly wake-minded', and in 1722 the family moved to Edinburgh so that he and his brother John could study at Edinburgh University. Hume matriculated at Edinburgh University in 1723 at the age of 12 – this was younger than was usual but not exceptionally so.

There he acquired a grounding in the classical authors, logic and metaphysics, natural philosophy, ethics and mathematics. In his brief autobiography 'My Own Life' (1993b:351–6) he describes this period of his life thus:

> I passed through the ordinary course of education with success, and was seized very early with a passion for literature, which has been the ruling passion of my life, and the great source of my enjoyment. My studious disposition, my sobriety, and my industry, gave my family a notion that the law was a proper profession for me, but I found an insurmountable aversion to everything but the pursuits of philosophy and general learning; and while they fancied I was poring over Voet and Vinnius, Cicero and Virgil were the authors I was secretly devouring.
>
> (1993b:351)

Hume left Edinburgh University without taking a degree and abandoned his half-hearted study of law by 1729 when he embarked upon the philosophical study that was to lead to his writing of *A Treatise of Human Nature* (1978). In Hume's own words he 'entered upon a new scene of Thought' and pursued it with such intensity that it led to a breakdown in his health, one result of which was a remarkable letter Hume wrote to an unnamed physician, probably John Arbuthnot, in which he described his symptoms in clinical terms and explained how a ravenous appetite transformed him in six weeks from 'a tall, lean and rawboned youth to the most sturdy, robust, healthful-like fellow you have ever seen, with a ruddy complexion and cheerful countenance' (1993a:348) – the familiar figure of the famous Allan Ramsay portraits. Hume's illness also had a significant effect on his mind. Though he had 'scribbled many a Quire of Paper' containing nothing but his own inventions, his illness made him incapable of 'reducing these to words' and copying 'the parts in order', and so delivering his opinions with 'such elegance and neatness as to draw the attention of the World' (1993a:349).

In the hope that a period of alternative employment would enable him subsequently to resume his philosophical studies with renewed vigour, in 1734 Hume took up a post as a merchant's clerk in Bristol, but he soon quarrelled with his employer and left for France to continue study and writing. There he lived first at Rheims and then at La Flèche, the small country town containing the Jesuit college in which Descartes had been educated. There, by 1737, he completed the *Treatise*. Hume then returned to London to find a publisher, and the *Treatise* was published anonymously, with Books 1 and 2 appearing in 1739, and Book 3 following in 1740 along with an 'Appendix' which contained some corrections to and modifications of his already published material.

The reception of the *Treatise* was far from being what Hume had hoped for. It 'fell *dead-born from the press*', he wrote, 'without reaching such distinction as even to excite a murmur among zealots' (1993a:352). This largely hostile and uncomprehending reception – on which Hume's anonymous publication of (what is now generally accepted by scholars to be) his own 'Abstract' in 1740 had no effect, despite its brilliant survey of the main lines of his argument – left Hume bitterly disappointed.

Between 1739 and 1745 Hume lived at Ninewells and began the attempt to make a greater impact on the literary world than the *Treatise* had produced. In 1741 and 1742 two volumes of *Essays, Moral and Political* appeared. These met with some success and in 1745 Hume applied unsuccessfully for the chair of Physical and Pneumatical Philosophy at Edinburgh University. His irreligious reputation was the cause of his failure to be appointed, and the controversy caused him to publish another anonymous pamphlet 'A Letter from a Gentleman to his Friend in Edinburgh', in which he defended himself against the charge of irreligion in a way that it is hard now not to see as disingenuous.

In 1745 Hume took up a post as tutor to the mad Marquess of Annandale. He spent a year in the post but was dismissed in 1746. He then acted as secretary to General St Clair, one of his relations, during two missions, one which was supposed to be a raid on the French in Canada but was downgraded to an abortive raid on the coast of France, and a second which took him to Vienna and Turin.

This period from 1745 to 1748 at least aided Hume's financial position and also gave him the time to rework the material of the *Treatise* into what he hoped would be a more accessible form. In 1748 the

Philosophical Essays Concerning Human Understanding (later called *An Enquiry Concerning Human Understanding*) appeared, under Hume's own name. This was a rewriting of Book 1 of the *Treatise*, in a more elegant form, with significant omissions and one significant addition (Section 10, 'Of Miracles', which probably contained material originally intended for the *Treatise* but was excised when Hume hoped to gain the recommendation of Bishop Butler).

In 1751 *An Enquiry Concerning the Principles of Morals*, Hume's revision of Book 3 of the *Treatise*, was published; the work which he described as incomparably the best of his writings. He also published *Three Essays Moral and Political* (1748) and *Political Discourses* (1752). In 1752 he again failed to secure a university appointment, being rejected for the Chair of Logic at the University of Glasgow. However, in the same year he was appointed to the post of Keeper of the Advocates' Library, a post in which he remained until 1757 and which provided him with the resources and opportunity to embark on his six-volume *History of England*, published in parts in 1754, 1756, 1759 and 1762. This, above all, established his literary reputation and ensured that he was better known in his time as 'David Hume, historian' than 'David Hume, philosopher'. During this time Hume also wrote the *Dialogues Concerning Natural Religion* (the main target of which was the teleological argument for God's existence), which he did not publish in his lifetime, presumably out of a concern not to add to his irreligious reputation, and the *Natural History of Religion*, which he did publish in 1757 (as part of his controversial *Four Dissertations*) though he can hardly have thought its approach would endear him to the religious authorities. In the same year, Hume resigned the post of Keeper of the Advocates' Library, having been found guilty of ordering indecent books (one of which was the *Contes* of La Fontaine) and unworthy of a place in a learned library.

In 1763 he went to Paris, as private secretary to Lord Hertford, the British ambassador. He was lionized by the French literary establishment, was a favourite of the fashionable ladies and developed friendships with Diderot, D'Alembert, d'Holbach, Helvetius, Buffon and (unfortunately for Hume) Rousseau. On Hume's return to England in 1766, Rousseau (who was fleeing from persecution in Switzerland) accompanied him. Later Hume was forced to defend himself in print against Rousseau's unjust accusations arising out of the relationship between them at this time.

Between 1767 and 1769 Hume was Under-Secretary of State, Northern Department, and from then until his death lived with his sister Katherine in Edinburgh. During these years he corrected his *History* for new editions, and continued to work on his *Dialogues*. His philosophical work had now attracted sufficient attention for him to be abusively attacked by James Beattie, a pupil of Thomas Reid (1710–96), whose work was successful enough to drive Hume to a public disowning of the *Treatise* as a 'juvenile work' and to an insistence that only the *Enquiries* should be regarded as expressing his opinions. Later philosophers, of greater perception than Beattie, have appreciated that to follow Hume's advice would be to ignore a masterpiece.

Finally, on his deathbed, Hume composed his brief autobiography 'My Own Life', published in 1777. In this, his final word on the matter, he refers to the lack of success of the *Treatise* as 'proceeding more from the manner than the matter' (1993b:352). He died from bowel cancer in 1776, at peace and (as he says in his autobiography) 'detached from life', considering that 'a man of sixty five, by dying, cuts off only a few years of infirmities'. His only expressed regret was that he could not now live to enjoy his growing literary fame (1993b:356).

The structure of Book 1 of the *Treatise* and its place in Hume's work

Hume describes his intention in writing *A Treatise of Human Nature* in the subtitle as 'An attempt to introduce the experimental method of reasoning into Moral Subjects'. Here 'Moral' is used in its wide eighteenth-century sense of 'pertaining to what is specifically human'; in the 'Advertisement' to Books 1 and 2, at the beginning of the *Treatise*, he writes:

> *My design in the present work is sufficiently explained in the* introduction. *The reader must only observe, that all the subjects I have planned out to my self, are not treated of in these two volumes. The*

> *subjects of the* understanding *and* passions *make a complete chain of reasoning by themselves; and I was willing to take advantage of this natural division in order to try the taste of the public. If I have the good fortune to meet with success, I shall proceed to the examination of* morals, politics *and* criticism; *which will compleat this* Treatise of human nature.

Hume thus intended a five-volume work, in which the experimental method of reasoning would be applied successively to the five aspects of human nature comprised in the subjects of the understanding, the passions, morals (in the narrower and still current sense), politics and criticism. But the work as we have it is in fact divided into three books: on the understanding, on passions and on morals. The public reception of the *Treatise* not being what Hume had hoped for, he abandoned his original plan and, as we have seen, attempted to gain a literary reputation by other means.

Book 1, 'Of the Understanding', is the most intensively studied and (as is generally acknowledged) the most difficult and intellectually ambitious of all Hume's writings. It is concerned with the origin of our 'ideas', the material of our thoughts, and the character and limitations of our intellectual activity. It is divided into four parts and each part into sections.

In Part I Hume introduces the basic vocabulary and principles he will be appealing to throughout the rest of his work. His exposition is brief and can seem fairly casual. But this is because he takes himself in the main to be going over ground which will be familiar to his readers and already adequately covered by John Locke. He does not merely follow Locke, however. He begins with a terminological innovation, introducing the term 'perception' to denote the basic elements of his system, the items which are 'before the mind' whenever any mental activity is going on. He divides perceptions into 'impressions' (corresponding to feeling or experience) and 'ideas' (corresponding to thinking). He also distinguishes between 'simple' and 'complex' perceptions. With this terminological apparatus in hand, Hume is then able to formulate the most fundamental principle of his system: the so-called Copy Principle, the principle that every simple idea must be a copy of (that is, must resemble and be causally derived from) a simple impression. It is this that defines him as an empiricist. It states a limit, or rather two limits, on what can be thought. First, that whatever can be thought of must be in some sense *encounterable* in experience (for ideas, the elements of thought, must resemble impressions, the elements of feeling) and, second, that thought can only be of that which *has already been encountered* in experience, or is in some sense *constructible out of what has already been encountered* in experience (since simple ideas must be the effects of simple impressions and causation runs from earlier to later). The Copy Principle thus sets Hume a task and provides him with an intellectual weapon. The task is to account for all the ideas that we have in a way that is consistent with it. The role of the Copy Principle as a weapon is described by Hume himself in the 'Abstract' of the *Treatise*:

> when he [Hume] suspects that any philosophical term has no idea annexed to it (as is too common) he always asks *from what impression that pretended idea is derived?* And if no impression can be produced, he concludes that the term is altogether insignificant.
>
> (1978:649)

The role of the Copy Principle in the *Treatise* is thus a complex one: Hume's acceptance of it constrains him to search for an account of the origin of such important, yet (in his view) problematic, ideas as space, time, identity, external existence, necessary connection and the self, but enables him to reject philosophical accounts of these ideas which do not conform to the Copy Principle (as is the case, for example, with the account of the self as a simple substance with which all of us are immediately acquainted in our own experience). A second division within the class of perceptions which Hume draws in Part I is that between perceptions 'of sensation' and perceptions 'of reflection'. This division is again drawn from Locke and does not loom large in Part I, and one might be tempted to dismiss it as an unnecessary piece of intellectual jumble. But its significance for Hume becomes clear in Part III, where it turns out to be a crucial component in his account of the origin of the idea of necessary connection – in fact, the idea of necessary connection turns out to be an idea of reflection.

Another division Hume makes in Part I is that between ideas that are general, or abstract, and those that are particular. Again this is a division made by Locke, but Hume rejects Locke's account of abstract ideas and endorses and elaborates instead that of Berkeley, according to which 'all general ideas are nothing but particular ones, annexed to a certain term, which gives them a more extensive signification, and makes them recall upon occasion other individuals, which are similar to them'. Hume ranks Berkeley's theory very highly, describing it as 'one of the greatest and most valuable discoveries that has been made of late years in the republic of letters' (1978:17). The significance of Berkeley's account for Hume can be seen by recalling again the self-imposed constraint of Hume's Copy Principle – it turns out that the only way Hume is able to account for our ideas of space, time, existence and, indeed, causation is as Berkeleian abstract ideas.

Three other fundamental elements of Hume's philosophy are introduced in Part I. The first is the Separability Principle, which Hume states as follows:

> Whatever objects are different are distinguishable, and whatever objects are distinguishable are separable by the thought and imagination.
>
> (1978:18)

The second is the Conceivability Principle:

> Whatever is clearly conceiv'd may exist, and whatever is clearly conceiv'd, after any manner, may exist after the same manner.
>
> (1978:233)

Or, more briefly:

> Nothing of which we can form a clear and distinct idea is absurd and impossible.
>
> (1978:19)

Together the Separability Principle and the Conceivability Principle imply that if any two objects are distinct they can exist separately – either can exist without the other. And it is this consequence Hume appeals to in rejecting the possibility of real connections between distinct existences, which rejection in turn underpins his rejection of necessary connections between causes and effects, his rejection of the notion of substance (except as applicable universally to anything that can be conceived) and his rejection of a simple self distinct from its perceptions.

The final fundamental element of Hume's thought introduced in Part I is his statement of his three principles of the association of ideas: resemblance, contiguity, and cause and effect. These (he believes) account for the order in which our ideas follow one another in our minds, and are also involved in the explanation of our coming to have beliefs in matters of fact beyond our memory and senses and in the origin of the problematic ideas already mentioned.

Part I of Book 1 of the *Treatise*, therefore, despite its brevity, is of fundamental importance in Hume's thought and underpins the argument of the rest of the first book.

In Part II of Book 1 ('Of the Ideas of Space and Time'), Hume attempts to provide an account of the ideas of space and time consistent with the principles outlined in Part I, and also discusses the ideas of existence and external existence. He begins his discussion by arguing against the infinite divisibility both of the ideas of space and time and of space and time themselves. His arguments are difficult, generally thought to involve fallacies and are not evidently relevant to the main lines of thought developed in the rest of Book 1 of the *Treatise*. (In the *Enquiry Concerning Human Understanding* the discussion is omitted.) But what Hume eventually arrives at is an account of the ideas of space and time as abstract ideas, derived from the 'manners of appearance' in which our perceptions array themselves in spatial and temporal relations: 'As 'tis from the disposition of visible and tangible objects we receive the idea of space, so from the succession of ideas and impressions we form the idea of time' (1978:35). Of these ideas the second, that of time, is of vital importance in Hume's later account of the idea of identity as a fiction of the imagination, which in turn is employed both in his account in Part IV of our belief in an external world and in his account of our belief in an enduring self.

The other important discussion in Part II is Hume's account of our ideas of existence and external existence, that is, existence independent of the mind. The former is identified by Hume as an abstract idea, not distinct from the idea of that which we conceive to be existent, so that the idea of existence 'when conjoined with the idea of any object, makes no addition to it' (1978:67). Here we see Hume struggling to express in his own terms (before the advances in logic which alone made it possible to gain a proper appreciation of the notion) and within a framework of thought which anyway could not contain it, the insight encapsulated in the slogan 'existence is not a predicate', in essence that things do not divide into those that exist and those that do not.

Finally, Hume's brief account of external existence, which completes Part II, anticipates his extended discussion in Part IV, to which he refers the reader. Here he insists that we can have no idea of anything 'specifically different from' (1978:67) – that is, wholly unlike – ideas or impressions, and propounds his dictum:

> To hate, to love, to think, to feel, to see, all this is nothing but to perceive.
>
> (1978:67)

This hints (by the use of the transitive verb 'perceive') at a central feature of his position: namely his reification of perceptions – his conception, that is, of being in a mental state as standing in a certain *relation* (of perceiving) to an *object* distinct from oneself.

By contrast with Part II, Part III ('Of Knowledge and Probability') is the most discussed of the four parts of Book 1 and contains some of Hume's most celebrated arguments. Its topic is the explanation of our belief in the existence of a world beyond our senses and memory. What, Hume seeks to know, accounts for our inference from the observed to the unobserved? Because of the way he approaches this problem Hume is led into a discussion of the notion of cause and effect, and the resultant Humean account of causation has remained a paradigm of philosophical analysis ever since. Its fundamental contention is that though the idea of necessary connection *is* an essential component of our idea of the cause–effect relation, there is no necessary connection between the things we call causes and effects themselves, so that '[a]ny thing can produce any thing' (1978:173), and any thing can fail to produce any thing. The idea of necessary connection is, in fact, copied from a feeling that arises when a transition is made in thought from the idea (or impression) of the cause to the idea of the effect. And our mistaken belief that causes and effects are themselves necessarily connected is a 'fiction of the imagination', which results from the mind's 'propensity to spread itself on external objects' (1978:167) – that is, to regard as features of the external world features that, in fact, belong only to the mind's perceptions. Our belief that every event *must* have a cause is to be explained similarly, Hume asserts. It is not in fact a *necessary* truth (though Hume never doubts that it is a truth) that every event, or every beginning of existence, has a cause.

Apart from his account of causation and his rejection of the necessity of a cause to every beginning of existence, Part III is also notable for what has often been taken to be the formulation by Hume (in Section 6) of what has come to be known as 'the Problem of Induction'. When we infer to the unobserved from the observed, as when we infer from the past to the future, is our procedure rationally justified, in the sense that our beliefs about the observed provide us with evidence for our beliefs about the unobserved? Whether Hume does pose this question in Section 6 and, if so, whether he answers it, are questions which are now much debated among Hume scholars. The question Hume himself formulates is the following:

Whether we are determined by reason to make the transition [from an observed cause to its effect], or by a certain association and relation of perceptions?

(1978:88–9)

His answer is emphatic:

Not only our reason fails us in the discovery of the ultimate connection of causes and effects, but even after experience has informed us of their *constant conjunction*, 'tis impossible for us to satisfy ourselves by our reason, why we should extend that

11

experience beyond those particular instances which have fallen under our observation.

(1978:91–2)

Whether Hume thus reveals himself to be a sceptic about induction is a matter we shall be looking into later.

Whatever should be said about this matter, however, the importance of scepticism in Hume's thought cannot be denied. Part IV of Book 1 ('Of the Sceptical and Other Systems of Philosophy') contains Hume's detailed exposition of, and response to, scepticism. Its first section ('Of Scepticism with Regard to Reason') contains an argument that reasoning – whether it be what Hume calls 'demonstrative', as in arithmetic or logic, or merely 'probable', as in inferences from cause to effect – can never give the slightest grounds for belief. The argument is generally considered to be fallacious, but it indicates how far Hume is prepared to follow the sceptical trail and is one he himself takes very seriously in his final assessment of scepticism in the concluding section of Part IV.

The second section of Part IV ('Of Scepticism with Regard to the Senses') contains Hume's discussion of the nature and causes of our belief in an external world. In this section Hume distinguishes two versions of our belief in an external world or 'body' – as he phrases it, the 'vulgar' or common-sense version and the 'philosophical' version. According to the vulgar version of the belief in an external world, our perceptions *themselves* have a distinct and independent existence. But Hume argues that this version of the belief, which is a product of the imagination, not of the understanding or reason, is false. The experiments which demonstrate this, lead philosophers to accept the philosophical version of the belief, a system of 'double existence' according to which, while perceptions have no independent existence, there are other items which do. But, Hume asserts, this philosophical version of the belief in body has no primary recommendation either to reason or to the imagination. It is simply a position into which philosophers are driven when they recognise the untenability of the vulgar view, but it is without rational warrant of any kind. Moreover it too is false, as Hume argues in the subsequent Section 4 ('Of the Modern Philosophy'), though he insists that nonetheless a belief 'in body' in some form is one 'we must take for granted in all our reasonings' (1978:187).

Part IV also contains, in Section 6, Hume's discussion 'Of Personal Identity', in which the object is again to explain our possession of a *false* natural belief: the belief in the existence of a unitary enduring self. The mechanism of the imagination which explains this belief is the very same as that which accounts for our belief in body: it is a mechanism which involves our mistakenly coming to think of related objects as *identical*. Since the idea of identity is already a 'fiction of the imagination' – an idea which, strictly speaking, has no application at all – the mechanism of the imagination which produces our beliefs in an external world and an enduring self thus involves, according to Hume, *two* levels of confusion.

Not surprisingly, therefore, Hume himself is prepared to say (in the 'Abstract') that 'the philosophy contain'd in this book is very sceptical' (1978:657). In the final section of Part IV, Hume attempts to put the scepticism of the *Treatise* into focus and assess the relationship of his philosophy to traditional scepticism. His general position – that the preceding parts of the *Treatise* show both the irrefutability and practical insignificance of philosophical scepticism – he perhaps expresses best in the 'Abstract':

Almost all reasoning is there [in the *Treatise*] reduced to experience and the belief, which attends experience, is explained to be nothing but a peculiar sentiment, or lively conception produced by habit. Nor is this all, when we believe anything of *external* existence, or suppose an object to exist a moment after it is no longer perceived, this belief is nothing but a sentiment of the same kind. Our author insists upon several other sceptical topics; and upon the whole concludes, that we assent to our faculties, and employ our reasoning only because we cannot help it. Philosophy would render us entirely *Pyrrhonian* were not nature too strong for it.

(1978:657)

However, the cool detachment of this summary gives little indication of the complexity and passionate intensity of the final section of Book 2. Here Hume, beginning in 'despair' and fancying himself 'some strange uncouth monster, who not being able to mingle and unite in society, has been expelled from all human commerce, and left utterly abandoned and disconsolate' (1978:264), eventually arrives at a position he can live with only by resolving to pursue philosophy in a 'careless manner' (1978:273), diffident towards his philosophical doubts as well as his philosophical convictions, and prepared to regard philosophy as something to be engaged in when the inclination takes him, and to be abandoned without regret when, and for so long as, his bent of mind turns away from it to the pleasures of everyday life.

It is hard not to read this section of the *Treatise* without seeing it as expressing, not merely a theoretical solution to a theoretical problem, but the *practical* lesson that Hume had learnt from his own recent breakdown about the way he must conduct his own life in order to control the 'melancholy and indolence' to which he found himself to be susceptible when the 'intense view of the manifold contradictions and imperfections in human reason' caused him to be overwhelmed by doubts and scruples (1978:268–9).

Book 1 of the *Treatise* contains Hume's discussion of ideas. Books 2 and 3 go on to discuss impressions of reflection, 'those other impressions ... called secondary and reflective, as arising from the original impressions or from their ideas' (1978:276). As for the original impressions (or 'impressions of sensation') which, without any antecedent perception, arise in the soul 'from the constitution of the body, from the animal spirits, or from the application of objects to the external senses' (1978:275) – the study of these, Hume says, 'belongs more to anatomists and natural philosophers than to moral' (1978:8). Thus Hume regards the *Treatise* in its entirety as discussing all the elements of the mental world which are the proper objects of study for the moral philosopher.

After the *Treatise*, as we have already noted, Hume restated and, to an extent that Hume scholars hotly debate, revised the matter of Book 1 in the *Enquiry Concerning Human Understanding*. Two differences between Book 1 of the *Treatise* and the *Enquiry* which are uncontroversial may be noted. The first is, in the latter, the much greater focus on causation as the chief topic and the brevity of the discussion of the sceptical arguments of Part IV of the *Treatise*. (The argument of

Section 1 of Part IV is dropped completely and the discussion of scepticism with respect to the external world – the topic of Sections 2 and 6 of Part I – is reduced to its bare essentials.) This shift in focus is already heralded, however, in the 'Abstract', in which the argument concerning causation is identified as the chief argument of the book. The second evident difference between Book 1 of the *Treatise* and the *Enquiry* is the role assigned to the principles of association in the former. The principles of association are not repudiated in the *Enquiry*, but Hume's enthusiasm for them is reduced – certainly from the degree indicated in the 'Abstract', in which his use of them is said to be that in the *Treatise* which 'if any thing, can intitle the author to so glorious a name as that of an *inventor*' (1978:661).

Another notable difference between Book 1 of the *Treatise* and the *Enquiry* is the omission from the latter of any discussion of personal identity. But this difference is accounted for by the 'Appendix', in which Hume states himself dissatisfied (for reasons that he does not make clear) with his discussion of the topic in Book 1, and declares the whole matter 'a labyrinth' (1978:633).

In other respects the *Enquiry* most obviously differs from Book 1 of the *Treatise* by addition, rather than by omission. In particular, it contains the two sections 'Of Miracles' and 'Of a Particular Providence and of a Future State'. But the former was probably originally intended for the *Treatise* itself, and the latter contains no change in Hume's philosophical position. What the two sections do is to make quite clear the irreligiosity of Hume's position, no doubt after it had become clear to him that his attempt in the *Treatise* to render his work inoffensive to religious opinion had failed.

The place of the *Treatise* in the history of philosophy: precursors, influences and effects

Hume, as we have already noted, was a voracious reader of philosophical literature. It will be useful here to consider briefly some of the writers whose work probably contributed most significantly to the development of his thought, and then to go on to look at his relation to his philosophical successors.

First among Hume's precursors to be mentioned, of course, must be Locke and Berkeley, his British empiricist predecessors. Locke is referred to five times in the infrequent footnotes to Book 1 of the *Treatise*, Berkeley only once (in the section 'Of Abstract Ideas') but in terms which clearly indicate what Hume considers to be the depth of his indebtedness to him.

The general position they have in common with Hume, which is the justification of the standard grouping of the three as 'the British empiricists', is expressed by Locke in these words in his *An Essay Concerning Human Understanding* (1961):

> Let us then suppose the mind to be, as we say, white paper, void of all characters, without any *ideas*. How comes it to be furnished? Whence comes it by that vast store which the busy and boundless fancy of man has painted on it with an almost endless variety? Whence has it all the materials of reason and knowledge? To this I answer in one word, from *experience*.
>
> (*Essay* II, i.2)

Berkeley writes:

> It is evident to any one who takes a survey of the objects of human knowledge, that they are either ideas actually imprinted on the senses, or else such as are perceived by attending to the passions and operations of the mind, or lastly ideas formed by help of memory and imagination, either compounding, dividing, or barely representing those originally perceived in the aforesaid ways.
>
> (1949:41)

Hume gives the most succinct statement of the position in his Copy Principle:

> All our simple ideas in their first appearance are derived from simple impressions, which are correspondent to them and which they exactly represent.
>
> (1978:4)

The genetic empiricism expressed in these passages is, then, an undoubted trait common to Locke, Berkeley and Hume; we shall need to look at it very carefully in what follows.

How much more, in the detail of his arguments, Hume owed to the other two is a matter of controversy. Clearly, in his discussion of personal identity, Hume had to have had Locke's groundbreaking account in mind, though how closely his discussion is intended as a response to Locke can be debated. (It is arguable, however, on the basis of textual comparison, that Hume must have had Locke's *Essay* before him, open at the relevant section, throughout the writing of his discussion of personal identity.) Berkeley's influence on Hume's discussion of abstract ideas has already been noted. The extent of his influence in other areas – Hume's discussions of space and time, and of the external world, for example – is more controversial, one scholar famously suggesting at one point that Hume had never even read Berkeley (Popkin 1964). But Hume's general attitude to Berkeley is made clear in a footnote in the first *Enquiry*:

> most of the writings of that very ingenious author form the best lessons of scepticism, which are to be found either among the ancient or modern philosophers, Bayle not excepted. ... [T]hat all his arguments, though otherwise intended, are, in reality, merely sceptical, appears from this, *that they admit of no answer and produce no conviction.*
>
> (1975:155)

From a self-avowed sceptic, the praise could not be more fulsome, and that Hume describes Berkeley's arguments as producing no conviction (albeit admitting of no answer) should not mislead us into thinking it at all qualified – this, after all, is exactly what Hume thinks will be true of his own arguments.

Another undoubted influence on Hume was Newtonianism. Newton's *Philosophiae Naturalis Principia Mathematica* was published in 1687 and his fame spread quickly thereafter. Hume would have encountered Newtonian science at Edinburgh during his university years, and would have had ample opportunity during the period of voracious reading he undertook thereafter to go further into the Newtonian system of ideas. And, in fact, in his *History of England* Hume refers to Newton in the most complimentary terms. In the *Treatise* itself Hume never refers explicitly to Newton by name, but it is impossible to miss the deliberate allusion in his description of the principles of association of ideas as 'a kind of ATTRACTION, which in the mental world will be found to have as extraordinary effects as in the natural, and to show itself in as many and as various forms' (1978:12–13). That Hume, in attempting to introduce the experimental method of reasoning into moral sciences, saw himself as attempting to do for the world of human thought what he perceived Newton as having already done for the physical world, is evident. The extent of the gap between the aspiration and the achievement (the extent of the difference between the precise mathematical formulation of Newton's theory of gravitational attraction and Hume's statements of the manner in which the principles of association constitute a 'gentle force' (1978:10) accounting for the non-randomness of our thought processes) is perhaps the explanation of the apparent loss of enthusiasm for the principles of association in Hume's writings after the *Treatise*.

The importance of the influence of Francis Hutcheson (1694–1747) on Hume was argued by Norman Kemp Smith in his monumental *The Philosophy of David Hume*. Kemp Smith writes:

> The thesis which I propose to maintain is that it was these contentions [Hutcheson's contentions that all moral and aesthetic judgements rest not on reason or on reflectively considered empirical data, but solely on feeling] which opened out to Hume 'the new Scene of Thought' of which he speaks in his letter of 1734. For there is a path that leads directly from them to all that is most fundamental in his philosophy.
>
> (1941:41–2)

Kemp Smith in fact speculated that in order of composition Books 2 and 3 preceded Book 1, noting that – in the treatment of association in Book 3 – 'association by causality is illustrated exclusively by those examples of blood and social relationship which are required for the purposes of Hume's argument in Books 2 and 3' (1964:245).

Hutcheson was an exponent of a 'moral sense' theory of ethics. He held that there was an inner sense which enabled us to discern good and evil. This inner sense was a feeling and did not rest on reason. Thus our judgements of good and evil are not based on reason, but feeling. Hume's ethics clearly parallels Hutcheson's. Section 2 of Part I of Book 3 is entitled 'Moral Distinctions Derived from a Moral Sense'. 'Morality', Hume writes, 'is more probably felt than judged of. ... To have the sense of virtue is nothing but to feel a satisfaction of a particular kind from the contemplation of a character. The very feeling constitutes the praise or admiration' (1978:470–1). And the title of Section 1 of Part I is 'Moral Distinctions not Derived from Reason' (1978:485).

What is controversial is the extent of Hutcheson's influence on Book 1 of the *Treatise*. Kemp Smith's belief in the importance of this influence is part of his account of Hume's philosophy as a form of *naturalism*, one which involves the thorough subordination of reason to feeling. The assessment of the justice of this description has been a preoccupation of Hume scholars ever since Kemp Smith's book was published and will be considered later.

If Hume's philosophy is not to be described as naturalism then another possibility is to describe it as scepticism; and since this is Hume's own self-description, it must in some sense be correct. In this connection the relationship of Hume to the sceptics of antiquity and to the great French sceptic Pierre Bayle (1647–1706) needs to be considered.

The relationship of Hume's philosophy to ancient scepticism has been much debated by modern scholars and is clearly of great significance. Hume refers to two schools of ancient scepticism: the Pyrrhonian and the Academic, rejecting the former and endorsing (in the *Enquiry*, 1975:61) the latter. The Pyrrhonist movement (founded by Aenesidemus when he broke away from the Academy during the first century BC) took its name from an earlier philosopher, Pyrrho of Elis, who was reported to have secured happiness through putting his scepticism into practice. This practical aspect of their scepticism was very important to the Pyrrhonists.

What we know about the Pyrrhonists we know mostly through the writings of a later member of the school, Sextus Empiricus (late second century AD). His texts *Outlines of Pyrrhonism* and *Against the Mathematicians* provide a summary of Pyrrhonist teaching. They began to be intensively studied in the fifteenth and sixteenth centuries and were translated into Latin in the 1560s. They provided most of the stimulus for the concern of early modern thinkers with scepticism.

Sextus defines scepticism as follows in his *Outlines of Pyrrhonism*:

> an ability, or mental attitude, which opposes appearances to judgements in any way whatsoever, with the result that owing to the equipollence of the objects and the reasons thus opposed, we are brought firstly to a state of mental suspense and next to a state of 'unperturbedness' or quietude.
>
> (1933–49: vol.1, p.8)

This definition identifies the three elements in Pyrrhonism which are relevant to Hume's understanding of it and his attitude towards it: the opposing of appearances and judgements, the suspension of judgement and the consequent state of tranquillity or unperturbedness.

The Pyrrhonian activity of opposing appearances and judgements, and generally of opposing to every proposition an equal proposition to force a 'dogmatist' to suspend judgement, is illustrated by Sextus in various examples. Thus, if someone says that a tower is square he is reminded that it only appears so from nearby and appears round from a distance. Again, the dogmatist who asserts that the existence of Providence is proved by the order of the heavenly bodies is confronted by the argument that the fact that often the good fare ill and the evil fare well disproves the existence of divine Providence. The Pyrrhonists made no claims of originality for such arguments; what they did claim originality for was the use to which they put them – not to establish any position, but rather to show that no position was more worthy of acceptance than any other and so to create a suspension of judgement.

Suspending judgement for the Pyrrhonists meant living without belief (*dogma*), but the Pyrrhonist does not deny appearances. As Sextus explains:

we do not overthrow the affective sense-impressions which induce our assent involuntarily; and these impressions are 'the appearances'. And when we question whether the underlying object is such as it appears we grant the fact that it appears, and our doubt does not concern it but the account given of that appearance.

(1933–49: vol.1, p.19)

There is much debate about the distinction drawn here between the passive assent to appearances of which Pyrrhonists approve and the belief or dogmatizing which they reject. But it is clear that the Pyrrhonists thought themselves entitled, despite suspending judgement, to engage in all the normal activities of life. As Sextus writes: 'Adhering, then, to appearances, we live in accordance with the normal rules of life, undogmatically, seeing that we cannot remain wholly inactive' (1933–49: vol.1, p.17). Sextus is here responding to the challenge, repeatedly made by opponents of Pyrrhonism, that a life without belief is unliveable. This objection was the heart of Hume's own rejection of Pyrrhonism: without belief there is no basis for action. Whether the Pyrrhonists had an adequate response to it is a matter of current controversy among scholars.

The third notion central to the Pyrrhonist philosophy is that of tranquillity (*ataraxia*). According to Sextus such tranquillity is a consequence of suspension of judgement (*epochē*). But that it is so is not a philosophical conclusion but a chance discovery. The first sceptic, Sextus says, set out to achieve *ataraxia* by determining the truth or falsity of competing judgements. But confronted with arguments of equal weight he was led to suspend judgement, and 'there followed, by chance, mental tranquillity in matters of opinion', *ataraxia* supervening on *epochē* 'as a shadow follows its object' (1933–49: vol.1, p.26). This is again a point on which Hume disagrees with the Pyrrhonists. The perplexity resulting from opposing appearance to judgement (or, in Hume, the imagination to reason), he thinks gives rise not to tranquillity, but to a 'sensible uneasiness' (1978:205) from which the mind 'naturally seeks relief' in a rejection of one of the two opposing principles. In the absence of such a resolution of the contradiction, the consequence is not tranquillity but 'despair' (1978:264).

The other form of ancient scepticism with which Hume was acquainted (and which he endorsed) was Academic scepticism, which was also the form of scepticism to which Cicero (106–43 BC), Hume's favourite ancient author, was most sympathetic. The most important figure in the history of Academic scepticism was Carneades (214–129 BC) and the primary target of his sceptical outlook was the 'cataleptic impressions' of the Stoics which were veridical and self-guaranteeing and provided a criterion of truth. Thus the Academic sceptics rejected the possibility of certain knowledge, but their scepticism was not as radical as that of the Pyrrhonists. In practical life Carneades proposed a theory of probability as a guide to life. He distinguished three levels of probability: the probable; the probable and undisputed; and the probable, undisputed and tested. According to Cicero these probabilities provide the Academic philosopher 'with a canon of judgement both in the conduct of life and in philosophical investigations and discussion' (1933:509): they show how life can be lived and judgements justifiable even though our claims are never immune to the possibility of error. In Part III of Book 1 of the *Treatise*, after the arguments about cause and effect which have been so often read as the clearest indication of Hume's scepticism, there occur three sections on probability and a section on 'Rules by which to Judge of Causes and Effects', and in the 'Abstract' of the *Treatise* Hume writes:

> The celebrated *Monsieur Leibniz* has observed it to be a defect in the common systems of logic, that they are very copious when they explain the operations of the understanding in the forming of demonstrations, but are too concise when they treat of probabilities and those other measures of evidence on which life and action entirely depend, and which are our guides even in most of our philosophical speculations. ... The author of the *Treatise of Human Nature* seems to have been sensible of this defect in these philosophers, and has endeavoured as much as he can to supply it.
>
> (1978:646–7)

A further important influence on Hume's thought in general, and on his scepticism in particular, was the great French sceptic, Pierre Bayle. Hume was well acquainted with Bayle's writings before he wrote the

Treatise, as we know from his early memoranda (Mossner 1948) and Bayle's great *Dictionnaire historique et critique* was an important mine of ideas and information for him. Apart from the general influence exerted by Bayle on his understanding and treatment of scepticism, two places in Book 1 of the *Treatise* where Bayle's influence is particularly visible are the discussion of space, time and vacuum in Part II, and Section 5 of Part IV in which Hume argues that the hypothesis of an *immaterial* soul substance is no more intelligible than that of a *material* soul substance.

The evidence of the influence of Bayle on Hume's discussion concerning space, time and vacuum is textual. Comparison of Hume's text with Bayle's article 'Zenon D'Elée' reveals similarities too great to be accidental (Kemp Smith 1941:284–90, 325–81). Bayle's aim in his discussion is sceptical: to show the unintelligibility of the notion of extension, and therewith that of the notions of space and time. Hume's purpose is to defend the intelligibility of these notions, as abstract ideas, and he does so in direct response to Bayle's arguments.

In his discussion of the hypothesis of the immateriality of the soul Hume uses arguments from the article in Bayle's dictionary on Spinoza, in the course of a teasing comparison which is intended to show that the theologians' 'doctrine of the immateriality, simplicity and indivisibility of a thinking substance is a true atheism, and will serve to justify all those sentiments, for which Spinoza is so universally infamous' (1978:240).

Of all the topics discussed in Book 1 of the *Treatise* perhaps the most important is causation, and in this connection the influence of Nicolas Malebranche (1638–1715) is crucial (for an extended investigation – to which the summary below is greatly indebted – see McCracken 1983). Some indication of the importance of Malebranche for Hume is indicated by the instructions he gave to his friend Michael Ramsey, shortly after completing the manuscript of the *Treatise*, concerning the course of preparatory reading Ramsey should undergo before attempting it. Ramsey should, Hume urged,

read once over the Recherche de la Verité of Père Malebranche, the Principles of Human Knowledge by Dr Berkeley, some of the more metaphysical Articles of Bayle's Dictionary; such as those

[on] Zeno, and Spinoza, Des-Cartes Meditations would also be useful but don't know if you will find it easily among your Acquaintances. These books will make you easily comprehend the metaphysical Parts of my Reasoning and as to the rest, they have so little Dependence on all former systems of Philosophy, that your natural Good Sense will afford you Light enough to judge of their Force and Solidity.

(Complete letter reprinted in Popkin 1964:774–5)

In Book 1 of the *Treatise* Malebranche is mentioned by name twice: in Section 14 of Part III ('Of the Idea of Necessary Connexion') and in Section 5 of Part IV ('Of the Immateriality of the Soul'). The text to which the former reference is attached provides convincing evidence of the attention with which Hume read Malebranche. Arguing for his conviction that the power by which a cause produces its effect is perfectly unknowable, Hume writes:

There are some, who maintain, that bodies operate by their substantial form; others by their accidents or qualities; several, by their matter and form: some by their form and accidents, others by certain virtues and faculties distinct from all this.

(1978:158)

Malebranche writes:

There are philosophers who maintain that second causes act by … their substantial form. Many by Accidents and Qualities, some by Matter and Form, others by Form and Accidents, others still by certain virtues, or of qualities distinct from all this.

(Malebranche 1700:156, quoted in McCracken 1983:257)

Evidently, as McCracken (1983:258) asserts, Hume not only had Malebranche's *Search after Truth* in mind as he wrote on causation, but he even had it open for consultation while writing.

Malebranche was an occasionalist. He denied that anything was a true cause except the infinite will of God. Anything else, however constantly conjoined with any other object, is a mere secondary cause or occasion on which the one true cause, divine power, acts to bring about its effect. The argument which Malebranche gives for this doctrine starts from his definition of a true cause: 'A true cause as I understand it is one such that the mind perceives a necessary connection between it and its effect' (Malebranche 1980:450, quoted in McCracken 1983:261). But, Malebranche insists, there is never perceivable such a necessary connection between any two *finite* beings. Therefore, it is only God who is a true cause since it is a contradiction that He should will and that what He wills should not happen. No finite will is connected in this way to what we are disposed to regard as its effect because there is no contradiction in the supposition that the event be willed and not occur. Similarly no other finite object is connected in this way to any other finite object because there is no contradiction, given any two finite objects, in the thought that one exists and the other not. Thus in the whole of the created world there is no true causal connection.

We are, of course, disposed to think differently, and to suppose that we can see that this is not the case. Indeed, we are inclined to think that we can *see* the force in one body communicated to another. But, Malebranche asserts, we are mistaken in this belief:

> Your eyes, in truth, tell you, say, that when a body at rest is struck by another it begins to move. ... But do not judge that bodies have in themselves some moving force, or that they can communicate such a force to other bodies when they strike them, for you see no such thing happen as that.
>
> (Malebranche 1968: vol.10, p.48, quoted in McCracken 1983:259)

The cause of our mistake is that a constant association of two things in our experience so acts on our brains as to create a habit of expectation, so that whenever we see one of the objects we form an expectation of the other; this habit of expectation, the work of the imagination, we mistake for a necessary connection between the two things, thus coming to believe that one is the true cause of the other. This, according to Malebranche, is why everyone concludes that a moving ball which strikes another is the true cause of the motion it communicates to the other, and that the soul's will is the true cause of movement in the arms – because it always happen that a ball moves when struck by another and that our arms move almost every time we want them to.

Hume, of course, was no occasionalist and made his opposition clear at every opportunity. But even given just this sketchy outline of Malebranche's views we can conclude that the extent of his agreement with Malebranche is considerable: like Malebranche he insists that in defining causation there is a necessary connection to be taken into account and so does indeed reject any mere regularity analysis of causation of the type that latter day 'Humeans' have put forward; like Malebranche he argues that no necessary connection can be discovered between any two finite things because there is no contradiction given any two distinct things, that one should exist and the other not; like Malebranche he denies that we can ever perceive the operation of any power or productive principle; like Malebranche he thinks, nevertheless, that we universally hold the mistaken belief that such finite items as the movements of two billiard balls are necessarily connected; and, finally, like Malebranche he explains this mistake as resulting from the operation of the imagination, acted on by experienced constant conjunctions, which creates a habit of expectation which the mind externalizes as a necessary connection between the constantly conjoined objects. Where Hume parts company with Malebranche is only in denying that his notion of 'true causation' has any applicability, and he does so (as he makes quite clear) only because he rejects innate ideas and, therefore, denies that we have any idea of God's will which can enable us to discover any more of a necessary connection between it and God's actions than between any finite will and the actions of its possessor. Thus he writes in the context of his discussion of the idea of necessary connection:

> the principle of inate ideas being allowed to be false, it follows that the supposition of a deity can serve us in no stead, in accounting for that idea of agency, which we search for in vain in all the objects, which are presented to our senses, or which we are internally conscious of in our own minds. For if every idea be derived from an impression, the idea of a deity precedes from the same origin; and if no impression, either of sensation or reflection,

implies any force or efficacy, 'tis equally impossible to discover or even imagine any such active principle in the deity. Since these philosophers [the occasionalists], therefore, have concluded, that matter cannot be endowed with any efficacious principle, because 'tis impossible to discover in it such a principle; the same course of reasoning should determine them to exclude it from the supreme being.

(1978:160)

Finally, in looking at influences on Hume's thought, we should not ignore Descartes (1596–1650): the philosopher customarily referred to in histories of philosophy as the first great Continental rationalist, as Hume is referred to as the last great British empiricist. Like Malebranche, Descartes is recommended to Michael Ramsey by Hume as useful preparatory reading for his study of the *Treatise*. The *indirect* influence of Descartes on Hume, through Malebranche (one of his followers) is undeniable, as we have just seen, but the extent of Descartes' influence is far greater than this indicates. As Thomas Reid wrote, Hume shared (along with Malebranche, Locke and Berkeley) a common 'system of the understanding' which 'may still be called the Cartesian system'.

The one great point of similarity between all these philosophers is their conception of philosophy as beginning with epistemology, the theory of knowledge. For all of them the primary question the philosopher must answer concerns the nature and limits of human knowledge. This conception of epistemology as the foremost part of philosophy is the most revolutionary element in Descartes' thought, and is the change in viewpoint which marks the beginning of what the textbooks call 'Modern Philosophy'. Descartes, unlike earlier philosophers, asked not just what the world is like, but how we can know what it is like. He thought also that he had provided an account of how this question could be answered, by starting from the one immediate, indubitable datum of consciousness he identified by the Method of Doubt – the *Cogito*, 'I think therefore I am' – and 'working out' to an external world via indubitable principles of inference (such as that the cause of an effect must have at least as much reality as the effect). His successors, however, found his appeal to such principles unconvincing and thus were left to confront the epistemological problem for themselves.

Hume refers to the Method of Doubt as a species of *antecedent* scepticism, scepticism antecedent to all study and philosophy, and explains his rejection of it in the first *Enquiry*. Such antecedent scepticism, 'inculcated by Des Cartes and others as a sovereign preservative against error and precipitate judgement', he says

> recommends an universal doubt, not only of all our former opinions and principles, but also of our very faculties; of whose veracity, say they, we must assure ourselves, by a chain of reasoning, deduced from some original principle, which cannot possibly be fallacious or deceitful.

But, he goes on,

> neither is there any such original principle ... above all others that are self-evident and convincing: Or if there were, could we advance a step beyond it, but by the use of those very faculties, of which we are supposed to be already diffident. The Cartesian doubt, therefore, were it ever possible to be attained by any human creature (as it plainly is not), would be entirely incurable; and no reasoning could ever bring us to a state of assurance and conviction on any subject.

(1975:149–50)

Hume here makes three criticisms of the Cartesian method. The first is that there is no principle which has the status Descartes assigns to the *Cogito*, the status of an indubitable truth, which cannot be fallacious or deceitful. The second is that even if there were such a principle, Descartes could not consistently proceed one step beyond it. The third is that the universal doubt Descartes suggests is not a possibility for the human mind.

The first of these criticisms can be elaborated, for Hume is not merely pointing to the logical gap between indubitability and truth. In Hume's view, it is not merely logically possible that there should be propositions it is impossible to doubt which are, in fact, false. This is actually the case, and can be proven to be so, he thinks, by irrefutable arguments ('arguments which admit of no answer and produce no conviction' (1975:155)). Such is the defective and fallacious nature of the human intellect. Thus, for Hume, indubitability provides no proof of truth; conversely, incredibility is no proof of falsehood.

Another point of difference between Descartes and Hume can be seen if we turn our attention from epistemology to metaphysics and philosophy of mind. Descartes maintained that the mind was an immaterial *substance* 'really distinct' from and independent of body, or material substance, and the notion of substance here is a fundamental concept for Descartes, as it is for his rationalist successors Spinoza (1632–77) and Leibniz (1646–1716). Hume decisively rejects it, and with it dualism in the Cartesian form. For the notion of 'substance' as independent existence, he claims, applies to everything that can be conceived, since there are *no* real connections and everything is, therefore, 'really distinct' (in Descartes' sense) from everything else. 'Substance' is, therefore, at least an empty term (and consequently of no use to anyone) and possibly a meaningless one. The mind, in particular, is not an immaterial substance, but a 'bundle of perceptions' and the Cartesian 'I' is a fiction. Thus, whether or not Hume's basic principles are Cartesian, the position he finally arrives at could not be more radically opposed to that of Descartes. His position is, in fact, the final stage in the development of empiricist thought about substance, beginning with Locke's uneasiness with the notion of an unobservable 'something, we know not what' underlying the observable qualities in things, followed by Berkeley's emphatic rejection of the notion of *material* substance and his attempted accommodation of the concept of the substantial self under the guise of a 'notion' rather than an idea. In this respect Hume's position marks the final emancipation of modern philosophy from that dependence on the Aristotelian and scholastic sources on which Descartes' philosophy was perceived by his successors to rest so unconvincingly.

Finally, a third point of contrast between Descartes and Hume in respect of their attitudes to non-human animals should be noted. Descartes notoriously held that non-human animals were merely automata, without souls, whose behaviour could be given a purely naturalistic, even mechanistic, explanation. Man, on the other hand, could never be completely part of the natural world because he possessed free will and reason. Thus, distinctively human thought and behaviour is forever beyond the possibility of natural explanation. Hume, by contrast, insists that all human life is naturalistically explicable and, emphatically rejecting Descartes' view of them as mere automata, insists that we can speak as legitimately of the 'reason' of animals as we can of that of man. 'No truth appears to me more evident than that beasts are endowed with thought and reason as much as men' (1978:176). In both the *Treatise* and the first *Enquiry* he has a section entitled 'Of the Reason of Animals', and in both he insists on a 'touchstone, by which we may try every system in this species of philosophy':

> when any hypothesis, therefore, is advanced to explain a mental operation, which is common to men and beasts, we must apply the same hypothesis to both; and as every true hypothesis will abide this trial, so I venture to affirm, that no false one will be ever able to endure it.
>
> (1978:177)

His 'own system concerning the nature of the understanding' (that is, that our reasonings are merely the products of experience operating on us, by means of custom alone), he argues, receives an 'invincible proof' when put to this test, for though it is sufficiently evident when applied to man, 'with respect to beasts there cannot be the least suspicion of mistake' (1978:178).

There could be no clearer indication of Hume's rejection of Descartes' position, both with respect to what is to be allowed as a form of argument by which conclusions about the nature of the human mind can be drawn, and with respect to the conclusion that is to be arrived at.

So far in this section we have been looking at the relation of Hume to his predecessors, but in order to appreciate fully Hume's philosophical importance we need also to attend to his relation to his successors. Despite Hume's disappointment at the reception of the *Treatise* his philosophy subsequently became more widely read and in Britain attracted, as well as a great deal of abuse, the respectful attention of Thomas Reid. But by far the most important effect of Hume's philosophy as it is set out in Book 1 of the *Treatise* and in *An Enquiry Concerning Human Understanding* was to wake Immanuel Kant, as he himself put it, from his 'dogmatic slumber' (1977:5) and to stimulate him to write his *Critique of Pure Reason*. In Kant's view, Hume was the first philosopher ever to identify the serious difficulties facing any attempt at metaphysics: 'since the origin of metaphysics so far as we know its history, nothing has ever happened which could have been more decisive to its fate than the attack made upon it by David Hume' (1977:3).

The particular stimulus to Kant's awakening was Hume's treatment of causation and his denial of any necessary connection between cause and effect. Kant describes Hume's achievement as follows:

> He challenged reason, which pretends to have given birth to this concept of herself, to answer him by what right she thinks anything could be so constituted that if that theory be posited, something else must necessarily be posited, for this is the meaning of the concept, of cause. He demonstrated irrefutably that it was entirely impossible for reason to think a priori and by reason of concepts such a combination as involves necessity. ... Hence he inferred that reason was altogether deluded with reference to this concept.
>
> (1977:3)

Kant thought that Hume was right to think that knowledge of particular causal connections could not be known a priori, that is, could only be discovered in experience. However, he thought that Hume went wrong in supposing that this was true also of the *general* Causal Maxim that everything has some cause. In Kant's view this *was* a necessary truth, knowable a priori. Nonetheless, Kant accepted Hume's view that the Causal Maxim was not something whose denial was self-contradictory; he insisted that it was not true simply in virtue of conceptual relationships, or the meanings of words, and so (in the now current terminology he introduced) a 'synthetic', rather than an 'analytic', truth. Hence, he claimed, the causal principle was a 'synthetic a priori' truth. And as such, Kant thought, it was representative of all metaphysics. For metaphysics properly so-called consists, he thought, of nothing but a priori synthetic principles and so the possibility of metaphysics becomes the question: 'How are a priori synthetic propositions possible?' (1977:21). It is to answering the question of the possibility of metaphysics framed in this way that Kant's *Critique of Pure Reason* is devoted, a work aptly described by a modern commentator as 'of an intellectual depth and grandeur that defy description' (Scruton 1995:134).

So long as Kant was thought to have 'answered Hume', Hume's philosophy, despite its historical influence, could be thought of as superseded. But in the present century the logical positivists (most importantly, Carnap, Schlick and Ayer), partly under the influence of Ernst Mach, the great turn-of-the-century philosopher of science and polymath, rejected the Kantian philosophy of the synthetic a priori and reasserted Hume's empiricism. They took as the guiding principle of their philosophy the famous concluding paragraph of Hume's *Enquiry*:

> When we run over our libraries persuaded of these principles, what havoc must we make? If we take in our own hand any volume – of divinity, or school metaphysics, for example – let us ask, '*Does it contain any abstract reasoning concerning quantity or number?*' No. *Does it contain any experimental reasoning concerning matter of fact and existence?*' No. Commit it then to the flames, for it can contain nothing but sophistry and illusion.
>
> (1975:165)

Where they had advanced on Hume, they thought, was only in being able to marry his empiricism with the powerful new logic of Frege and Russell.

More specific influences of Hume on twentieth-century philosophy have been his formulation (as it were thought) of 'the Problem of Induction' – a form of sceptical problem wholly unknown to pre-Humean philosophy – and his response to the problem of personal identity, first formulated by Locke. The former has dominated twentieth-century philosophy of science; the latter has been the central strand in the still ongoing contemporary debate about personal identity and, under the influence of Derek Parfit's writings (especially Parfit 1986), has become increasingly the orthodox position.

Thus, Hume is a figure whose importance cannot be denied. Whether right or wrong, his influence brought about, through Kant, a revolution in the way philosophy was conceived (what Kant, in fact, called a 'Copernican revolution') and both his general approach and particular doctrines are still relevant to present-day philosophical debate.

Aims and methods

With the basic knowledge we now have of the arrangement of themes and arguments in Book 1 of the *Treatise*, it will be useful to look at Hume's own conception of his purpose as this is set out in the introduction to the *Treatise*. Then we shall examine, in a general way, the appropriateness of the main labels that have been applied to him: moral scientist, sceptic, naturalist and empiricist. Finally, we shall consider what value, if any, on a Humean view, philosophical activity can actually possess.

One of the most important features of Hume's philosophy is his explicitly stated intention to 'introduce the experimental method of reasoning into moral subjects'. In fact, in its subtitle the *Treatise* is described as 'an attempt' to do just this. In describing his enterprise in this way, Hume thought of himself as, in general, applying the Newtonian method to philosophy. The principles of the philosophical programme which follows from this are set out in the introduction to the *Treatise*. Hume begins, as many philosophers have done, by bemoaning the weaknesses to be found in all former philosophical systems:

> Principles taken upon trust, consequences loosely deduced from them, want of coherence in the parts, and of evidence in the whole, these are everywhere to be met with in the systems of the most eminent philosophers, and seem to have drawn disgrace upon philosophy itself.

(1978:xvii)

The truth of these charges, Hume maintains, is made evident to all by the general fact that there is:

> nothing which is not the subject of debate, and in which men of learning are not of contrary opinions. The most trivial question escapes not our controversy, and in the most momentous we are not able to make any certain decision. ... Amidst all that bustle, 'tis not reason, which carries the prize, but eloquence: and no man need ever despair of garnering proselytes to the most extravagant hypothesis, who has art enough to represent it in any favourable colours.
>
> (1978:xvii)

The most important reason for this unsatisfactory situation, according to Hume, lies in the sheer difficulty of dealing with arguments (such as those of metaphysics) which do not belong to any particular branch of science, and have caused so much lost labour in their pursuit. Nevertheless, Hume thinks, only 'the most determined scepticism, along with a great deal of indolence, can justify this aversion to metaphysics. For if truth is attainable at all 'tis certain it must lie very deep and abstruse and to hope to arrive at it without pains ... must certainly be esteemed sufficiently vain and presumptuous' (1978:xxviii–xxix). And he writes: 'I pretend to no such advantage in the philosophy I am going to unfold, and would esteem it a strong presumption against it, were it so very easy and obvious' (1978:xix).

To resolve these difficulties Hume introduces a thesis which he regards as basic to his philosophy and the key that will at long last open the door to the philosophical treasure chest: that all the sciences are related to and in some way dependent on the science of man, and that discoveries in the latter may therefore lead to a better understanding of, and improvement in, all areas of scientific endeavour. Hume's statement of this thesis is very bold:

> all the sciences have a relation, greater or less, to human nature; and that however wide any of them may seem to run from it, they still return back by one passage or another. Even *Mathematics*, *Natural Philosophy* and *Natural Religion*, are in some means

dependent on the science of MAN; since they lie under the cognizance of men, and are judged of by their powers and faculties. 'Tis impossible to tell what changes and improvements we might make in these sciences were we thoroughly acquainted with the extent and force of human understanding and could explain the nature of the ideas we employ and of the operations we perform in our reasoning.

(1978:xix)

The argument is that a science is a body of knowledge and the product of human intellectual activity. But since such activity involves the use of *ideas* in *reasoning*, we can come to a better understanding of the limits of – and possible degree of improvements in – any particular science, if through the science of man we can come to a better understanding of those two components of our thoughts.

Though bold, this thesis is hardly clear and the argument not very convincing – how, for example, might an advance in pure mathematics be the result of a better understanding of human nature? Hume, in fact, goes on to indicate his awareness of the relatively unconvincing nature of his general argument in the sentence immediately following, in which he distinguishes Natural Religion from the other sciences mentioned and points out that not only are we the creators of this science, as we are of all others, but we are also its subject-matter:

And these improvements are the more to be hoped for in Natural Religion, as it is not content with instructing us in the nature of superior powers, but carries its view further, to their disposition towards us, and our duties towards them, and consequently we ourselves are not only the beings, that reason, but also one of the objects, concerning which we reason.

(1978:xix)

Hume next proceeds to mention four other sciences of which human beings are the subject-matter and which can, therefore, be seen as dependent on the science of man in the same way as Natural Religion: Logic, Morals, Criticism and Politics:

35

The sole end of logic is to explain the principles and operations of our reasoning faculty, and the nature of our ideas, morals and criticism regarding our tastes and sentiments and politics consider men as united in society, and dependent on each other.

(1978:xix–xx)

In these sciences, then, advance is, Hume claims, dependent on the science of man, or the study of human nature, since their subject-matters are particular features of human nature. Moreover, Hume goes on to say, rather surprisingly in view of his high opinion of Newton, '[i]n these four sciences … is comprehended almost everything which it can in any way import us to be acquainted with, or which can tend either to the improvement or ornament of the human mind' (1978:xix–xx). The implication here that mathematics is neither of use nor ornament is understandable, since Hume himself was no mathematician, and the implied downgrading of Natural Religion is likewise comprehensible, since in Hume's view its status is merely that of a branch of pathology – a scientific study of one of the diseases to which mankind is prone. But that Hume should imply the insignificance of Natural Philosophy is remarkable. Perhaps he was allowing his rhetoric to run away with him.

However that may be, Hume is now in a position to put forward his own proposal for a solution to the endless perplexities which have beset philosophy so far:

To march up directly to the capital and centre of those sciences, to human nature itself; which once being master of, we may every where else hope for an easy victory. From this station we may extend our conquests over all those sciences, which more intimately concern human life, and may afterwards proceed at leisure to discover more fully those which are the objects of pure curiosity. There is no question of importance, whose decision is not compriz'd in the science of man; and there is none, which can be decided with any certainty, before we become acquainted with that science. In pretending, therefore, to explain the principles of human nature, we in effect propose a compleat system of the sciences, built on a foundation almost entirely new, and the only one in which they can stand with any security.

(1978:xx)

And, Hume goes on to say, as the science of man is the only foundation for all the other sciences, so experience and observation can provide the only foundation for the science of man. So Hume's aim is to extend the Newtonian method to human nature and to state the general laws which govern all human activities, basing these laws on experience and observation – that is, the experimental method. He says, in fact, that the subject is not entirely new, but has already been begun by some 'late philosophers' in England: 'Mr Locke, my Lord Shaftesbury, Dr Mandeville, Mr Hutcheson, Dr Butler etc.' (1978:xxi). But he suggests that these philosophers are to be compared to Lord Bacon, the original employer of the experimental method in natural philosophy:

'Tis no astonishing reflection to consider, that the application of experimental philosophy to moral subjects should come after that to natural at the distance of above a whole century; since we find, in fact, that there was about the same interval betwixt the origins of these sciences, and that reckoning from THALES to SOCRATES, the space of time is nearly equal to that betwixt my LORD BACON and some late philosophers in England, who have begun to put the science of man on a new footing.

(1978:xxi)

The implication of the analogy, if completed, is that Hume's work is to be the culmination of the application of the experimental method to the moral sciences as Newton's work was its culmination in the natural sciences.

As we have already seen, moreover, it is not just in its method that Hume intends his work to parallel Newton's. The science of man he conceives is intended to account for mental activity by reference to 'principles of union' which constitute a 'kind of ATTRACTION which will, in the mental world, be found to have as extraordinary an effect as in the natural' (1978:12–13). The analogue to the point-particles of Newton's physics on which gravity operates are Hume's simple ideas, and the interaction of these particles in accordance with the principles of association is, for Hume, the whole subject-matter of the science of man. As to the causes of the attraction constituted by the principles of association, Hume says these are things which

> I pretend not to explain. Nothing is more requisite for a true philosopher, than to restrain the intemperate desire of searching into causes, and having established any doctrine upon a sufficient number of experiments, rest content with that, when he sees a further examination would lead him into obscure and uncertain speculations.
>
> (1978:13)

The case is no different from that of natural philosophy, Hume thinks:

> the essence of the mind being equally unknown to us with that of external bodies, it must equally be impossible to form any notion of its powers and qualities otherwise than from careful and exact experiments. ... And ... 'tis certain we cannot go beyond experience, and any hypothesis, that pretends to discover the ultimate original qualities of human nature, ought at first to be rejected as presumptuous and chimerical. But if this impossibility of explaining ultimate principles should be esteemed a defect in the science of man, I will venture to affirm, that 'tis a defect common to it with all the sciences. ... None of them can go beyond experience, or establish any principles which are not founded on that authority.
>
> (1978:xxi–xxii)

The only difference between the two cases Hume will allow is that, in applying the experimental method to his subject-matter, the moral philosopher has a 'peculiar disadvantage' since in a psychological experiment if the experimenter makes himself his subject then his reflection and premeditation will disturb the operation of his natural principles, and render it impossible to form any just conclusions from the phenomenon. Hence, moral philosophers must 'glean up [their] experiments in this science from a continuous observation of human life, and take them as they appear in the common course of the world, by men's behaviour in company, in affairs and in their pleasures' (1978:xxiii).

So much for Hume's conception of his enterprise as he explains it in the introduction to the *Treatise*. With this in mind the justification for describing him as a 'moral scientist' is evident, but commentators frequently describe him also in other ways: sceptic, empiricist and naturalist, and one of the main problems in getting Hume's philosophy into focus is to see how or whether these various aspects of his thought interact and can be reconciled. We shall approach this issue by taking a preliminary look at the structure of Hume's discussion of the three main topics of Book 1 of the *Treatise*: causation and causal inference, our belief in an external world and personal identity.

First we need definitions of scepticism, empiricism and naturalism.

Scepticism consists in the belief that in some or all areas of everyday or scientific activity we lack the justification we ordinarily think that we have for our opinions. Scepticism may take a purely theoretical form, or it may take a prescriptive form by suggesting that, in view of the fact that our beliefs lack rational warrant, we should alter in some way how we think and act. Pyrrhonism, as we have seen, was a prescriptive form of scepticism, recommending (at least as interpreted by Hume) suspension of belief in all matters, and it was for this reason that Hume opposed it, denying both the possibility of such a response and its desirability.

Empiricism, as we have noted, is the outlook common to Locke, Berkeley and Hume. It consists, in brief, in the contention that sense experience is the source of all knowledge – 'nothing is in the intellect unless it is first in the senses'. It has two aspects: first, it denies that we can have any concepts or ideas which are not cashable in terms of experience – call this *content empiricism* – and, second, it denies that we can have any knowledge of matters of fact except through experience – call this *epistemological empiricism*.

Hume's content empiricism is expressed in his Copy Principle, the genetic thesis that all simple ideas are copies of simple impressions, which is his formulation of Locke's denial of innate ideas. Hume's endorsement of epistemological empiricism consists in his conjunction of two contentions about causation: the first, that knowledge of causation alone can provide us with a basis for inference to facts about the world which are not immediately accessible to our senses; the second, that knowledge of causation must itself be based on experience.

The first of these contentions Hume expresses in the *Treatise* in the following passages:

> 'Tis only causation, which produces such a connection, as to give us assurance from the existence or action of one object, that 'twas followed or preceded by any other existence or action.
>
> (1978:73–4)

> of these three relations, which depend not upon the mere ideas, the only one, that can be traced beyond our senses, and informs us of existences and objects, which we do not see or feel, is causation.
>
> (1978:74)

In the first *Enquiry* Hume formulates this contention more succinctly in the terminology of 'matters of fact' as follows:

> All reasonings concerning matter of fact seem to be founded on the relation of *Cause and Effect*. By means of that relation alone we can go beyond the evidence of our memory and senses.
>
> (1975:26)

The second contention – about the necessary basis of knowledge of causation itself – Hume rests on his fundamental claim that, since causes and effects are distinct existences and there are no necessary connections between distinct existences, only experience can provide us with any information about particular causal connections. In the words of the *Enquiry* once again:

> When … it is asked, *What is the foundation of all our reasonings and conclusions concerning* [the relation of cause and effect]*?* it may be replied in one word. Experience.
>
> (1975:32)

Naturalism, finally, is the contention that human activities are part of the natural world and are to be explained in the same way as other such activities. We have seen how sharply his acceptance of this position distinguishes Hume from Descartes. We have also noted Kemp Smith's claim that it was this naturalism, derived from Hutcheson and involving the thorough subordination of reason to feeling, which was intended by Hume as the major emphasis of his work.

Let us now see how these three themes interact in Hume's thought about causation, the external world and personal identity.

In each case we find the same pattern of argument. Hume first asks why we think as we do about the topic; that is, what our justification is for our ordinary belief. Why do we think of causes and effects as necessarily connected, and why do we think that their connection will continue in the future? Why do we think that the world exists when we do not perceive it? Why, even, do we think of ourselves as persisting through time with an identity which remains despite all the changes that take place in it? In each case, Hume argues, no reason can be given for these natural beliefs. In each case, in fact, philosophy provides irrefutable arguments against our natural beliefs. Philosophical arguments establish that there are no necessary connections between any events and hence no contradiction in supposing that events labelled 'causes and effects' associated in the past will not continue to be associated in the future. Equally, philosophical argument establishes that our natural belief that our perceptions are capable of a continuous and independent existence is both without any rational foundation and is, in fact, false. Again, philosophical arguments establish that our belief in personal identity is a belief in a fiction.

It is because he argues in this way that Hume is correctly thought of as a sceptic, and his scepticism is founded on his empiricism, specifically on his epistemological empiricism. We have just seen how Hume distinguishes (in the *Enquiry* in so many words, but the distinction is already there in the *Treatise*) between matters of fact, which can be justified only by causal reasoning from experience, and relations of ideas. The crucial next step in Hume's argument in each case is to claim that at this point, where experience alone can provide justification, it can also be seen to be insufficient. Hence *nothing* can justify the beliefs in question.

The case of the causal reasoning underlying our practice of forming beliefs about unperceived matters of fact on the basis of our experience is illuminating, though also rather special. In this case our particular beliefs based on causal reasoning *are* justified, Hume thinks: they are a product of reason, in the sense he uses the expression, and so are founded on 'just inference' (1978:89). However, our engagement in the practice of causal reasoning is not itself a product of reason, since to be so it would have to be a consequence of our rational acceptance of the proposition that 'those instances of which we have no experience, resemble those of which we have had experience'. But our acceptance of this proposition can be justified neither by demonstrative arguments (since its denial is not self-contradictory) nor, without circularity, by probable arguments – that is, arguments, based on experience, from cause to effect. For the only experience we can appeal to is past experience; but past experience can only justify beliefs about the future on the supposition that the future will be like the past. However, the supposition that the future will be like the past is a supposition about a matter of fact, and hence only justifiable by appeal to experience, but it is also a supposition about the future, and hence only justifiable by appeal to past experience on the supposition that the future will be like the past. Thus, since the only experience we can appeal to is past experience, though

> all our experimental conclusions proceed upon the supposition that the future will be conformable to the past ... to endeavour ... the proof of this last supposition by probable arguments, or arguments regarding existence, must be evidently arguing in a circle, and taking that for granted, which is the very point in question.
>
> (1978:30–6)

Hume argues similarly in the case of our other natural beliefs. In the case of our belief in an external world, he argues that neither our belief in its 'vulgar form' (that is, the form in which we all hold it prior to philosophical reflection and to which we all return when we are out of the study), nor our belief in its philosophical form, can be a product of reason, since in neither case can it be arrived at by just inference via causal reasoning, nor can it be a product of demonstrative reasoning. It is, in fact, a product of the imagination, understood in a narrow sense (1978:117), which Hume opposes both to demonstrative and to causal reasoning (for the importance of the distinction between the narrow and broad senses of the imagination in the *Treatise*, see Loeb 1991, 1995a and 1995b, to which I am greatly indebted). The mechanism of narrow imagination generates the belief in an external world via the influence of two features of our experience: the constancy and the coherence of our perceptions, of which the former is more important. Our belief in its natural form is the primary product of this mechanism and is certainly false. The philosophical form of the belief in an external world, which is a belief in the double existence of perceptions and objects, is a secondary product of the imagination, which philosophers are led to when they realise the falsehood of the vulgar form of the belief and which could only be arrived at by someone who was predisposed to the vulgar belief. Like the vulgar belief, however, it has no recommendation to reason and, in fact, is opposed by it, so that it is not 'possible for us to reason justly and regularly from causes and effects, and at the same time believe in the continued existence of matter' (1978:266).

The status of our belief in an enduring self is similar. In fact, it is exactly the same mechanism of the imagination, in the narrow sense, which produces the beliefs in an external world and the belief in an enduring self. The difference is only that in the case of the self Hume makes no distinction between vulgar and philosophical forms of the belief. The primary product of the imagination in this case is thus a belief in an enduring self distinct from our perceptions. But this belief is a 'confusion and mistake', whose function is merely 'to disguise the variation in our perceptions' and 'justify to ourselves [the] absurdity', to which we have a great propensity, of thinking of our distinct perceptions, however interrupted or variable, as in effect one and the same (1978:254).

The movement to scepticism via epistemological empiricism is thus a prominent line of thought in Hume, but there is also another line of thought which connects his scepticism with his content empiricism. As a content empiricist Hume's position is that a genuine belief must involve concepts applicable to and, in fact, derived from experience. However, in some cases Hume thinks that no foundation in experience can be found for a putative concept at all, and we talk without meaning if we pretend otherwise. In the 'Abstract', as already noted, Hume describes his procedure in a way which highlights this conceptual scepticism:

> whenever any idea is ambiguous he [Hume] always has recourse to the impression which must render it clear and precise. And, when he suspects that any philosophical term has no idea annexed to it (as is too common) he always asks from what impression the pretended idea is derived? And if no information can be produced he concludes that the term is altogether insignificant.
>
> (1978:648–9)

Thus Hume operates with a criterion of meaningfulness by appeal to which he is able to condemn philosophical flights of fancy and to set a limit to the legitimate content of common-sense belief. As the passage from the 'Abstract' indicates, it is when he is discussing philosophical fancies rather than common-sense beliefs that this concern with meaningfulness is uppermost. But it also figures, for example, when he argues not only that our common-sense belief in a unitary self is merely an unwarranted product of the imagination, but also that it is meaningless since no impression of such a self (that is, no experience of such a self) could ever be available to provide content for the idea. In fact, in Hume's thought, the meaningfulness both of talk about the external world and talk about enduring selves is suspect for a deeper reason. In both cases our imagination works to generate the belief in question via the production of a (propensity to) a false belief in the identity of related (causally linked or resembling) perceptions. However, for Hume the idea of identity is itself a fiction of the imagination which he describes thus: 'an idea, which is a medium betwixt unity and number; or more properly speaking, is either of them, according to the view in which we take it' (1978:201). As the grammar of this passage indicates, properly speaking there are just the two ideas: unity and number. There is no idea of identity distinct from these, and thus no beliefs, true or false, in the identity or otherwise of related perceptions. In general, then, Hume is prepared to argue on the basis of his empiricism that our fundamental everyday beliefs and practices are without rational warrant, that is, incapable of being supported either by demonstrative or probable (causal) reasoning. In some cases they are contrary to reason (as is the case with the belief that matter continues to exist unperceived (1978:266)); in some cases just false (as is the case with the vulgar form of the belief in an external world and our belief in a necessary connection between those distinct events labelled by us as 'causes and effects'), and they are even, in some cases, meaningless.

But Hume does not rest with these sceptical conclusions. The scepticism is characteristically just the first outcome of the first, negative, phase of his investigation. Next, Hume goes on to explain why we think as we do, by appeal to the natural tendencies of the human mind together with certain features of our experience. Nature, he claims, has not left it to our choice, in such matters of fundamental importance, what to believe, and has 'esteemed it an affair of too great importance to be trusted to our uncertain reasonings and speculations' (1978:187). There are 'principles of the imagination' – psychological mechanisms by which belief is produced – which are 'permanent, irresistable and universal ... the foundation of all our thought and action, so that upon their removal human nature must immediately perish and go to ruin' (1978:225). These include 'the customary transition from causes to effects, and from effects to causes' (so that Hume is here using 'imagination' in a larger sense (1978:118) which includes reason), but they also include those mechanisms of belief foundation, belonging to the imagination in the narrow sense, which account for our belief in the necessary connections of the events we label 'cause' and 'effect', and our belief in an external world and an enduring self; these principles, too, are 'equally natural and necessary in the human mind' (1978:226) although in some circumstances 'directly contrary to' the customary transition 'from causes and effects' (1978:264). Thus we are compelled by our nature, given the course of our experience, to believe in the necessary connection of causes and effects, the existence of an external world and the persistence of an enduring self, even though we can give no rational foundation for these beliefs, and even though they can all be

opposed by rational argument. It is in this way that Hume is fundamentally opposed to the Pyrrhonist philosophy.

Seen in this way Humean scepticism and naturalism go hand in
hand. The scepticism rules out one type of explanation of our
everyday beliefs and practices – that they are the products of reason –
and the naturalism provides another – that they are the products of
(narrow) imagination. Nevertheless, there is evidently a tension
between them. For the core of Hume's response to scepticism is
simply that it is incredible and that once we leave the study

> to dine, to play a game of backgammon, to converse, to be merry
> with friends – when we would return to these speculations, they
> appear so cold and strained and ridiculous, that I cannot find it in
> my heart to enter into them any further.
>
> (1978:269)

Given this contemptuous attitude which we naturally take, once we
leave the study, towards philosophy and the scepticism to which it
leads, why should we engage in it at all? And how can Hume maintain
his evident preference for the philosophical views of mind and reality,
to which we are led by the transitions in thought from cause to effect
and effect to cause which he regards as properly belonging to reason,
over the common-sense view, to which we are led by the equally
natural and necessary principles which, he insists, belong only to the
imagination narrowly conceived?

It is not evident that these questions have any complete answers.
But the first point to note in response to them is that it *is* possible, for
a short time, in the seclusion of one's study, genuinely to come to
doubt what one naturally believes when engaged in everyday activities, and the pursuit of philosophical, and therefore sceptical, lines of
enquiry is just as natural a disposition of the mind as its propensity to
its natural beliefs. Some people, not including all of mankind, and in
particular not including many honest gentlemen in England
(1978:272), but including Hume, have a natural disposition to philosophy, and there is no reason why such a disposition should not be
indulged:

At the time, therefore, that I am tired with amusement and company, and have indulged a *reverie* in my chamber, or in a solitary walk by a river-side, I feel my mind all collected within itself, and am naturally inclined to carry my view into all those subjects, about which I have met with so many disputes in the course of my reading and conversation. I cannot forbear having a curiosity to be acquainted with the principles of moral good and evil, the nature and foundation of government and the cause of those several passions and inclinations which actuate and govern me. I am uneasy to think that I approve of one object, and disapprove of another, call one thing beautiful, and another deformed, decide concerning truth and falsehood, reason and folly, without knowing on what principles I proceed. I am concerned for the condition of the learned world, which lies under a deplorable ignorance in all these particulars. I feel an ambition to arise in me of contributing to the instruction of mankind, and of acquiring a name by my inventions and discoveries. These sentiments spring up naturally in my present disposition, and should I endeavour to banish them, by attending myself to any other business or diversion, I feel I should be a loser in point of pleasure; and this is the origin of my philosophy.

(1978:270–1)

But philosophical activity is not merely intrinsically pleasurable, it also has practical and beneficial results. It is true that the sceptical suspension of belief which philosophy dictates is necessarily temporary, and 'carelessness and indolence' inevitably draw us back into the common fold, but reflective philosophical activity can nevertheless produce significant change. Common sense does not simply reassert itself once we leave the study. For Hume the most important way in which this is true is that philosophical activity, and the awareness of the force of sceptical arguments to which it gives rise, affect us by making us more cautious and diffident, and equipping us with a greater sense of our fallibility. An awareness of 'the strange infirmities of the human understanding' can prevent people 'throwing themselves precipitately into opinions with no concern for opposing arguments' and 'naturally inspire them with more modesty and reserve, and diminish their fond opinions of themselves, and their prejudice against antagonists' (1978:129).

Finally, philosophical study, and the awareness of our cognitive limitations to which it leads, can persuade us that we should confine our speculations to the natural beliefs of common life and that the decisions of philosophy should be 'nothing but the reflections of common life, methodized and corrected'. Thus it can persuade us that we should abjure speculation about such matters as God, freedom and immortality, aware that the limitations of our cognitive powers are such that we could never hope to achieve, in these areas, any reasonable grounds of belief.

Further reading

For Hume's life, see Mossner, C.E. (1954) *The Life of David Hume*, Austin: University of Texas Press.

General works on Hume's philosophy include:

Basson, A.H. (1958) *David Hume*, Middlesex: Penguin Books.

Flew, A. (1986) *Hume: Philosopher of Moral Science*, Oxford: Blackwell.

Kemp Smith, N. (1941) *The Philosophy of David Hume*, London: Macmillan.

Stroud, B. (1977) *Hume*, London: Routledge & Kegan Paul.

Material particularly relevant to the themes of this chapter is contained in:

Berkeley, G. (1949) *The Works of George Berkeley*, vol.2, ed. A.A. Luce and T.E. Jessop, London: Thomas Nelson & Sons.

Cicero, M.T. (1933) *Cicero*, vol.19, trans. R.H. Rackham, Cambridge, MA: Harvard University Press, 28 vols.

Descartes, R. (1984) *The Philosophical Writings of Descartes*, vol.2, ed. and trans. J. Cottingham, R. Stoothoff and D. Murdoch, Cambridge: Cambridge University Press.

Fogelin, R. (1985) *Hume's Skepticism in the 'Treatise of Human Nature'*, London: Routledge & Kegan Paul.

Kant, I. (1977) *Prolegomena to Any Future Metaphysics*, Indianapolis: Hackett Publishing Company.

Locke, J. (1961) *An Essay Concerning Human Understanding*, ed. J. Yolton, London: Dent.

McCracken, C.J. (1983) *Malebranche and British Philosophy*, Oxford: Clarendon Press.

Malebranche, N. (1980) *The Search after Truth*, trans. T.M. Lennon and P.J. Olscamp, with a commentary by T.M. Lennon, Columbus: Ohio State University Press.

Mossner, C.E. (1948) 'Hume's Early Memoranda, 1729–1740: The Complete Text', *Journal of the History of Ideas* 9:492–518.

Norton, D.F. (ed.) (1993) *The Cambridge Companion to Hume*, Cambridge: Cambridge University Press.

Popkin, R.H. (1964) 'So, Hume Did Read Berkeley', *Journal of Philosophy* 61:774–5.

Reid, T. (1941) *Essays on the Intellectual Powers of Man*, ed. A.D. Woozley, London: Macmillan.

Scruton, R. (1995) *A Short History of Modern Philosophy*, London and New York: Routledge.

Chapter 2

Hume's theory of
the mind

The contents of the mind

In Part I of Book 1 of the *Treatise* Hume sets forth his
account 'Of ideas, their origin, composition, abstraction, connexion, etc.' This is his account of the nature
and origin of thought, which he intends to serve as the
foundation of his philosophy; it is taken largely from
Locke and assumed by Hume to be fairly uncontroversial. For this reason his account is brief – too brief to
satisfy commentators – and to a philosophically
informed modern reader obscure, since the concept of
an 'idea', which Hume and Locke employed with such
confidence, seems, in the light of subsequent philosophical progress and particularly after the work of
Wittgenstein, to be deeply problematic. But we can
only hope to understand the defects of the theory of
ideas if we first understand the theory itself, and to do
that we must begin where Hume began, with Locke.

Locke uses the term 'Idea' to stand for 'Whatsoever
the Mind perceives in itself, or is the immediate object of
Perception, Thought or Understanding' (*Essay* II,

viii.8). According to Locke, whenever any mental activity takes place ideas are 'before the mind' and are the 'direct objects' of the mind's awareness. This is so whenever we exercise any of our five senses in perception of the external environment, feel any sensation, think any thought or engage in any process of reasoning. Thus no mental activity can take place without the passage of ideas before the mind and the passage of ideas before the mind is all that is required for mental activity.

It is natural, today, to protest that Locke is ignoring a huge difference, the difference between perception and thought, in counting both as transactions with 'ideas'. What could be more different than *the sensory experience of seeing a tree*, and *the thought of a tree*, had in the physical absence of any tree, perhaps with one's eyes closed or in the dark? A modern philosopher is tempted, in reading Locke and Hume, to insist on an ambiguity: 'idea' can mean either 'content of a sensory experience' or 'exercise of a concept in thought'. But it cannot mean both.

However, in Locke it *does* mean both, for a crucial aspect of Locke's account is that it involves an *assimilation* of thought to perception, that is, a treatment of thinking as essentially a transaction with materials of the very same kind as are involved when perception takes place. It does so because Locke's intention is not only to explain what thought is, but also to explain its origin, and via the assimilation of thought and perception (or concepts and percepts) he is able to give a very simple account: *all* ideas are derived from experience.

But there are two types of experience – outer and inner – and correspondingly two types of ideas: *ideas of sensation*, which come into our mind by way of our senses, and *ideas of reflection*, which are the mind's representations of its own activities. Examples of ideas of sensation are:

> Those ideas we have of *yellow*, *white*, *heat*, *cold*, *soft*, *hard*, *bitter*, *sweet*, and all those which we call sensible qualities.

Examples of ideas of reflection are:

> *perception*, *thinking*, *doubting*, *believing*, *reasoning*, *knowing*, *willing*, and all the different workings of our own minds.

> (*Essay* II, i.3)

So Locke's fuller answer to the question 'Whence has [the mind] all the materials of reason and knowledge?' is:

> To this I answer in one word: from *experience*. In that all our knowledge is founded, and from that it ultimately derives itself. Our observation employed either about *external sensible objects or about the internal operations of our minds perceived and reflected on by ourselves, is that which supplies our understandings with the materials of thinking.* These two are the fountains of knowledge, from whence all the *ideas* we have, or can naturally have, do spring.
>
> (*Essay* II, i.2)

Locke's theory of ideas, then, has two elements: (1) an account of mental activity which assimilates perception and thought, and (2) a genetic component – an account of the origin of thought – which *limits* the thinkable to the already experienced or experienceable. But in order to defend the second component of this theory Locke needs another division within the class of ideas, which cuts across the division between ideas of sensation and ideas of reflection: namely, the division between *simple* and *complex* ideas. Simple ideas are those 'in the reception of which the mind is only passive' and are 'received from sensation and reflection' (*Essay* II, xix.1). The mind then performs various operations on these simple ideas which result in complex ideas, which can, in turn, be operated on. Thus, by its creative activity on simple ideas (Locke claims), the mind can generate all the materials of thought from those which it receives through sensation and reflection:

> even *the most abstruse ideas*, how remote soever they may seem from sense, or from any operations of our own minds, are yet only such as the understanding forms to itself by repeating and joining *ideas* that it had either from objects of sense or from its own operations about them: so that even large *and abstract ideas are derived from sensation or reflection*, being no other than what the mind, by the ordinary use of its own faculties employed about *ideas* received from objects or from the operations it observes in itself about them, may and does attain to.
>
> (*Essay* II, xii.8)

Since to think is to operate with ideas it follows that:

> the simple *ideas* we receive from sensation and reflection are the boundaries of our thoughts; beyond which the mind, whatever effort it may make, is not able to advance one jot, nor can it make any discoveries, when it would pry into the nature and hidden cause of these *ideas*.
>
> (Essay II, xxii.29)

Since we cannot know what we cannot think, knowledge, as well as thought, is limited to what can be derived from the senses.

In all this Hume follows Locke, but with some terminological changes and some modifications and change of emphasis. He calls all the 'objects of the mind' not 'ideas' but 'perceptions', distinguishing 'perceptions' into 'impressions' and 'ideas', and noting that in doing so he is 'restoring the word, idea, to its original sense, from which Mr *Locke* had perverted it, in making it stand for all our perceptions' (1978:2). Like Locke he distinguishes between perceptions of sensation and perceptions of reflection. Thus he makes a four-fold division between (1) impressions of sensation, (2) impressions of reflection, (3) ideas of sensation, and (4) ideas of reflection. Examples of these are (1) seeing a colour or feeling a pain, (2) feeling fear, (3) the thought of a colour or pain, and (4) the thought of fear. These enter the mind, according to Hume, in the order (1), (3), (2) and (4). Again, like Locke, Hume distinguishes between simple and complex ideas, and is thus able to adhere to the fundamental empiricist thesis that all knowledge derives from experience. But Hume does not recognise every idea-forming operation that Locke acknowledges and, in particular (as we shall see), not the operation of abstraction, and is thus more tightly constrained in his account of complex ideas than Locke. Another difference between Locke and Hume is that Hume does not accept the possibility of any necessary connection between simple ideas, whereas Locke does (*Essay* II, vii.7) and so some ideas which count as simple for Locke (*Essay* II, iii–vii) – extension and space, for example – are complex for Hume.

Two other points with respect to which Hume and Locke may be usefully compared are, first, the *ontological status* of ideas and, second, their *representational quality*. In many places Locke speaks of ideas as entities, 'the immediate objects' of the understanding. The impression given by his phrasing is that ideas are independently existing *things* with qualities of their own, to which the thinker or perceiver stands in a genuine relation (of 'grasping' or 'immediate perception') rather than mere states or properties of persons whose existence consists merely in their thinking or perceiving in certain ways. If so, we can enquire (1) what qualities do ideas have in themselves, independently of the relations they stand in to other things or we stand in to them, (2) what is the relation we stand in to ideas when mental activity takes place, and (3) what relations do ideas stand in to the things we ordinarily take ourselves to be perceiving or thinking about, the trees and dogs and houses and people we think of ourselves as encountering in our everyday transactions? Whether Locke is to be thought of as thus 'reifying' ideas is a matter of controversy among commentators, encapsulated in the debate as to whether Locke's account of sense-perception is an 'indirect realist' one.

According to what is perhaps the still most widely accepted interpretation of Locke's theory of perception, for a man to see a tree involves three things standing in suitable relations: a man, an idea of a tree and a tree. The man sees the tree if and only if the man perceives the idea which is caused by and resembles (in certain respects) the tree. Thus on this account our relationship to the things we ordinarily take ourselves to perceive is mediated by ideas which form a kind of veil between us and the external world.

According to an alternative account of Locke this is a mistaken interpretation. Thus John Yolton writes: 'I see no evidence in the *Essay* that Locke thought of ideas as entities' (1970:134); earlier he explains:

Having visual images *is* seeing objects, under specific conditions. The way of ideas is Locke's method of recognising mental features of seeing. It does not place the perceiver in some vale of ideas forever trying to break out into the world of physical objects.

(1970:132)

According to this account a person's 'perceiving an idea' is, for Locke, no more a genuine relation between the person and the idea than a person's being 'in' a mood is a genuine relation between the person and the mood (see Bennett 1971:31–5 for the development of this analogy). Certainly there are moods of various kinds and people can be in them. But moods are not things which it makes sense to suppose might exist independently of people being 'in' them and to which people might perhaps stand in other relations. Rather, moods are non-relational states *of* people. For a mood to exist *is* for a person to be 'in' it. Moods are *adjectival* on people in this sense: anything which can be sensibly said about moods can be paraphrased without using the noun and capturing the content of the statement in a clearly non-relational formulation. Thus, for a person to be in a happy mood is for a person to be happy, for a person to be in a sad mood is for that person to be sad, for a person to be in a short-lived happy mood is for that person to be briefly happy, and so on.

The same is true, *mutatis mutandis*, of Lockean ideas on the alternative interpretation. Certainly there are ideas of various kinds and people can have them. But ideas are not things which it makes sense to suppose might exist independently of being 'had' and to which people might, perhaps, stand in other relations. Rather, a person's having an idea is a non-relational state. For an idea to exist is for a person to 'have' it. In this sense ideas are adjectival on people, they have their ideas as they have their properties and anything which can sensibly be said about ideas can be paraphrased without using the noun and capturing the content of the statement in a clearly non-relational formulation.

It is unclear, as indicated above, which of these two interpretations of Locke's theory of ideas should be accepted, because Locke never directly confronts the issue. Hume, by contrast, makes his position on the ontological status of perceptions completely unambiguous. Hume reifies perceptions. He regards all perceptions as things – indeed as substances, in so far as that notion makes any sense – and the relation between perceiver and perception – that of perceiving – as a genuine relation holding between independently existing things (1978:233). Thus he accepts that perceptions are not adjectival on perceivers, that it makes sense to suppose that perceptions can exist independently of being perceived and that for a person to be in any psychological state is for a certain relational statement to be true of that person.

Or rather this is the position from which Hume starts. But once perceptions are considered as ontologically on a par with perceivers it is a short step to the conclusion that there is no perceiver apart from perceptions, so that there is, after all, no genuine relation of perceiving between perceiver and perception *qua* two independent things. Not, however, because perceptions are adjectival on perceivers, but rather because perceivers are *themselves* ontologically constituted out of perceptions – are 'bundles' of perceptions, as Hume puts it. As we shall see later it is, in fact, this line of thought, rather than any independently based thoughts about the unobservability of the perceiving self (as expressed in Hume's famous dictum 'I can never catch myself without a perception, and never can observe anything but the perception' (1978: 252)) that leads Hume to this conception of the self.

The second point of difference between Locke and Hume mentioned above concerned the representational quality of ideas/perceptions (see also Norton 1993:30). According to the Lockean account (at least as interpreted most straightforwardly with ideas reified as images), though the immediate objects of perception and thought are ideas, indirectly we can perceive and think of other things which our ideas represent. How we can know that there is anything outside of themselves which our ideas represent, is indeed a large problem for Locke – it is the problem of our knowledge of the external world – since according to Locke's account everything could be as it is within the mind and the external world be wholly different, or not there at all. Nevertheless, Locke thinks that we can be justified in thinking that there is an external world and that our ideas represent it.

But ideas represent in two ways. Some ideas represent via resemblance, as a painting of a cat might be said to represent a cat because the images and colours on the canvas bear a resemblance to those of a cat. Thus, Locke claims, the ideas of 'solidity, extension, figure, motion or rest and number' (*Essay* II, viii.9):

are *resemblances* of [these qualities], and their patterns do really exist in the bodies themselves ... a circle or a square are the same, whether in *idea* or existence, in the mind or in the [material world].

(*Essay* II, viii.15–18)

However, other ideas do not resemble anything in the material world. Ideas of colours, tastes, smells and so on, do not resemble their causes in the objects perceived. Rather their causes are best regarded as powers to produce the appropriate ideas in us, and there is not anything in the objects resembling the ideas produced. Thus in the case of these ideas representation is not via resemblance. Rather it is by causation:

though whiteness and coldness are no more in snow than pain is, yet those ideas of whiteness and coldness, pain, etc., being in us the effects of powers in things without us ... are real *ideas* in us whereby we distinguish the qualities ... in things themselves. ... These several appearances being designed to be the marks whereby we are to know and distinguish things which we have to do with, our *ideas* do as well serve to that purpose and are as real distinguishing characters, whether they be only constant effects or exact resemblances of something in the things themselves; the reality lying in that steady correspondence they have with the distinct constitutions of real beings ... it suffices that they are constantly produced by them.

(*Essay* II, xxx.2)

The distinction drawn here between those ideas which represent by resembling and those ideas which represent by causation is the distinction between ideas of primary qualities, which resemble their causes, and ideas of secondary qualities, which do not. The distinction makes it difficult for Locke to give an account of how ideas represent, but (as we have seen) he rises to the task and offers a bifurcated account to accommodate the complexities that the primary/secondary distinction brings with it.

Hume does not bother. He takes it to be a consequence of 'the modern philosophy' – that is, paradigmatically the Lockean philosophy – that the whole notion of perceptions representing external things has to be abandoned. For, he thinks, the principal conclusion of the modern philosophy that colours, sounds, tastes, smells, heat and cold are:

> nothing but impressions in the mind, deriv'd from the operation of external objects, and without any resemblance to the qualities of objects
>
> (1978:227)

can be derived from considerations which establish this conclusion as one which is 'as satisfactory as can possibly be imagined' (1978:228).
But:

> If colours, sounds, tastes and smells be really perceptions, nothing we can conceive of is possest of a real, continu'd and independent existence, not even motion, extension and solidity, which are the primary qualities chiefly insisted on.
>
> (1978:228)

The reality of motion depends upon that of extension and solidity (1978:228). And the idea of extension is of something composed of simple and indivisible parts which are either coloured or solid. But since, according to the modern philosophy, colour is excluded from any real existence, the reality of our idea of extension depends upon that of solidity. But 'our modern philosophy leaves us no just or satisfactory idea of solidity; nor consequently of matter' (1978:229). In fact, there is no impression and, therefore, no idea of solidity. For 'feeling is the only sense, that can convey the impression, which is original to the idea of solidity' (1978:230), but, in fact, the impressions of touch do not 'represent solidity nor any real object' (1978:231). Thus, Hume concludes, when we reason from cause and effect, as the modern philosophers do, the conclusion is 'that neither colour, sound, taste nor smell have a continu'd and independent existence' and 'when we exclude these sensible qualities there is nothing in the universe which has such an existence' (1978:231).

What he takes to be the Lockean picture of a world of external objects, possessing primary but no secondary qualities, and thus partly resembling our ideas, and causing both those of which it contains resemblances and those of which it does not, is consequently wholly rejected by Hume. Within his classificatory scheme ideas represent, and causally derive from, impressions, but impressions represent nothing. In particular this is so of impressions of sensation 'which arise from the soul originally, from unknown causes' (1978:7) – a comment whose significance does not emerge until some two hundred and twenty pages later, in the section 'Of the Modern Philosophy'.

Impressions and ideas

For Hume, then, his subject matter, as a moral philosopher, can only be our perceptions *qua* perceptions, and the distinctions and relations between them. And the first distinction Hume makes, from which everything else stems, is the division between impressions and ideas. This distinction, Hume says, corresponds to the distinction between *feeling* and *thinking*. ('Feeling' here refers to the kind of feeling constituted by any sense-experience, not merely the experience of touch – a visual sensation of colour, for example, is a feeling in Hume's sense; it also includes feelings of pain and pleasure, and passions and emotions.) But Hume also characterises it as a distinction between those perceptions 'which enter with most force and violence into the soul' and 'the faint images of these in thinking and reasoning'. Thus the difference between impressions and ideas for Hume is not a difference in kind but a difference in degree: a difference between *lively*, *vivid* or *forceful* perceptions and those which are fainter, less lively, vivid or forceful. That is to say, for Hume as for Locke, there is no difference of kind but only a difference of degree between what 'passes before the mind' when one sees a tree and when one thinks of a tree. How this can be so is explained within Hume's theory of mind by his thesis that ideas are faint *images* of impressions. Just as one can see a tree, so one can imagine – picture – a tree before one. Just as one can hear a tune played on a piano so one can imagine – or play through – the tune in one's mind. Now it seems right to say that there is something in common between what occurs in the former situation in each case and what occurs in the latter situation. What is going on in the one situation is different from, but like, what is going on in the other situation. Hume attempts to capture this difference using the vocabulary of 'liveliness' or 'vividness' or 'vivacity' or 'forcefulness', but he does not think that he is thereby *explaining* the difference. Rather he takes it to be a difference which everyone is acquainted with and so says 'it will not be very necessary to employ many words in explaining this distinction' (1978:1).

But now, if the difference between seeing a tree and forming an image of a tree in one's mind's eye *can* be characterised in this way, then the same must be true of the difference between seeing a tree and thinking of a tree *if thinking of something is merely to have an image of it in mind*. But this imagist theory of thought, derived from Locke, with all its attendant inadequacies, *is* Hume's theory of thought. Hence he is able to think, like Locke, that sensory perception and thinking are two activities which differ only in being transactions with entities – impressions in the one case and ideas in the other – which themselves differ only in respect of degree of a quality appropriately called 'vivacity', 'vividness', 'liveliness' or 'forcefulness'. Thus there are two places where criticism of Hume's distinction can focus: (1) on the contention that, for example, seeing a tree and forming an image of a tree in one's mind's eye differ in respect of something appropriately called 'vivacity', and (2) on the imagist theory of thinking, which may or may not be held along with the first contention.

Criticism of the imagist theory of thinking, deriving from Wittgenstein, we shall return to, but criticisms of the first of the two contentions just distinguished is harder to sustain, precisely because the notion of vivacity is a metaphor which Hume never attempts to cash. But there are two features of vivacity which are important to Hume. First, that the difference in degree of vivacity between impressions and ideas is always a phenomenological one. Impressions and ideas *appear* different and do not differ merely in their relations to other things, and (in particular) do not differ merely in their causal origin. Hume acknowledges that in particular instances 'they may very nearly approach to each other' (1978:2) and so be mistaken for one another, but even in such cases there is only a 'near resemblance' (1978:2). The second feature of vivacity which is important to Hume is that it is the very same quality which, by differing in degree, distinguishes belief from mere thought. This has to be so because his only account of belief is 'a lively (or vivacious) idea associated with a present impression' and his only explanation of how belief comes about is that vivacity is transmitted from an impression to an associated idea. Thus Hume's theory of the association of ideas, in its role as an explanation of the phenomenon of belief, comes to nothing unless the *same* notion of vivacity can be applied to impressions and beliefs.

The Copy Principle and the missing shade of blue

We shall come back to Hume's theory of the association of ideas. But first we must ask: if it is granted that impressions can be adequately distinguished from ideas, where do we get our ideas from? To this question, of course, Hume answers: they are copies of impressions. So they do not merely resemble impressions in virtue of being fainter versions of them; they are copies *of* impressions in the sense of being causally derived from them rather as a photograph is derived from its original.

The first important point to note about this thesis is that Hume represents it as an empirical discovery. He first notices that on a quick survey it looks as if, for every idea a man has, there is an exactly resembling impression and vice versa:

all the perceptions of the mind are double and appear both as impressions and ideas. When I shut my eyes and think of my chamber, the ideas I form are exact representations of the impressions I felt; nor is there any circumstance of the one, which is not to be found in the other. In running over my other perceptions, I find still the same resemblance and representation. Ideas and impressions appear always to correspond to each other. This circumstance seems to me remarkable, and engages my attention for a moment.

(1978:3)

But then he notes that on closer inspection this is a mistake:

Upon a more accurate survey I find I have been carried away too far by the first appearance, and that I must make use of the distinction of perceptions into *simple and complex*, to limit this general decision, *that all our ideas and impressions are resembling.* I observe, that many of our complex ideas never had impressions, that corresponded to them, and that many of our complex impressions never are exactly copied in ideas. I can imagine to myself such a city as the *New Jerusalem*, whose pavement is gold and whose walls are rubies, tho' I never saw any such. I have seen *Paris*; but shall I affirm I can form such an idea of that city, as will perfectly represent all its streets and houses in their real and just proportions?

(1978:3)

Hume concludes 'the rule is not universally true' that there is an exact correspondence between *complex* impressions and ideas but:

After the most accurate examination of which I am capable, I venture to affirm, ... that every simple idea has a simple impression, which resembles it; and every simple impression a correspondent idea.

(1978:3)

Hume emphasises that this conclusion is something that 'we find' (1978:4), a matter of observation of which anyone may 'satisfy himself' by 'running over' as many of his own simple ideas and impressions as he pleases. He then goes on to raise the question of 'how they stand with regard to their existence, and which of the impressions and ideas are causes, and which effects' (1978:6). He observes that such a constant conjunction as he observes between impressions and ideas never arises by chance, but is a 'proof' of causal dependence, and since impressions are always temporally prior in their occurrence to their corresponding ideas there is an 'equal proof' that our impressions are the causes of our ideas, not our ideas of our impressions (1978:5), since causes must precede their effects.

Thus Hume establishes the Copy Principle:

> All our simple ideas in their first appearance are deriv'd from simple impressions, which are correspondent to them and which they exactly represent ...
>
> (1978:4)

on the basis of observation, as a matter-of-fact discovery. Nor could it be otherwise on his conception of causation, for (as we shall see) it is of the essence of that account that there are no necessary connections between distinct existences and that *anything* can cause *anything*.

Thus when Hume immediately goes on, after formulating the Copy Principle, to note that there is one 'contradictory phenomenon' which may prove that "'tis not absolutely impossible for ideas to go before the correspondent impressions' (1978:5), he means more than that it is *conceivable* that this should happen. Rather, he means that it is in some sense an epistemic possibility, which we can have no reason to believe does not actually occur.

The 'one contradictory phenomenon' in question is the notorious shade of blue. Consider some particular shade of blue and imagine a man who has, as it happens, experienced all other shades of blue except this one. Would he not be able to supply it from his imagination, by arraying all the other shades of blue in a sequence and observing the gap in the spectrum where the missing shade would be? Yet the idea of the missing shade of blue, Hume insists, is a simple idea. So in this case, he claims, we can form a simple idea without any encounter with any corresponding simple impression – and, we may add, he does not think that this is a mere possibility, on a par with the sun's falling out of the sky, but something that for all we know actually occurs. Yet he is remarkably complacent: 'the instance is so particular and singular that 'tis scarcely worth our observing, and does not merit, that for it alone, we should alter our general maxim' (1978:6).

Commentators have found this attitude extremely puzzling, given the polemical manner in which Hume appeals to the Copy Principle to question the significance and validity of philosophical notions like substance and necessary connection. For if, in fact, there *can* be, and for all anyone knows *are*, simple ideas not preceded by corresponding simple impressions, how can Hume argue that a particular philosophical notion is bogus because there is no impression from which it is derived? If the missing shade of blue is a counter-example to the Copy Principle, then perhaps (an opponent could suggest) the same is true of the idea of 'necessary connection'. How, then, can Hume continue to use the Copy Principle *polemically* once he has admitted that it is false? Is his doing so really just, as H.A. Pritchard bad-temperedly wrote, a mere piece of effrontery on Hume's part towards his readers – 'and if he had considered the idea of cause as also to be ignored as being an isolated exceptional case, he would have had no reason to write the *Treatise* at all' (Pritchard 1950:177)? Or is there something more interesting to be said?

The Copy Principle and empiricism

To explore this question further we need first to get a better grip on the role of the Copy Principle in Hume's thought and the way in which it functions as an expression of his empiricism. We shall then see that there are two possible solutions to our puzzle, neither of which, however, because of the brevity of Hume's text, can be decisively endorsed.

First we need to note a further point about Hume's distinction between impressions and ideas. (Here and in the following exposition of the first possible solution I am greatly indebted to Bennett 1971: Chapter 9). As we have seen, his 'official' view is that (1) impressions and ideas differ only in respect of their degrees of forcefulness and vivacity, and (2) this difference corresponds to the difference between feeling and thinking. But he has a tendency, which is inconsistent with this, to equate impressions with the objects of veridical perceptual states. This tendency surfaces, for example, in his remark:

Everyone of himself will readily perceive the difference between feeling and thinking. The common degrees of these are easily distinguished, tho' it is not impossible but that in particular instances they may very nearly approach to each other. Thus in a sleep, in a fever, in madness or in any very violent emotion of the soul, our ideas may approach to our impressions.

(1978:1–2)

To remove the difficulty confronting him here, Hume need only have accepted that in sleep, fever or madness, *impressions* are before the mind, and his official way of distinguishing ideas from impressions gives him no reason not to do so. However, in so far as impressions are to be thought of as only involved in *veridical* perception, the non-veridical states involved in sleep, fever or madness cannot be so classified. Thus Hume's tendency to equate impressions with veridical sensory states is evidenced by his refusal to take what is apparently, given his 'official' view, the easy way out of the difficulty he here confronts.

Next we need to note another point. Hume holds that ideas are the constituents of thoughts, that is, are concepts. But for a language-user to employ a term with meaning is for the user to associate it with a concept. So Hume's account of *thought* doubles as an account of *linguistic understanding* and his account of the origin of ideas can be understood as a thesis about the preconditions of understanding – the thesis of *meaning empiricism*.

Putting these points together we can understand Hume's Copy Principle as entailing the thesis:

(A) A simple (indefinable) general term can only be understood if something which falls under it has been encountered in veridical sensory experience.

It is clear that Hume does take (A) to be part of his claim. One piece of evidence for this is his claim, in confirmation of the Copy Principle, that:

wherever by any accident the faculties, which give rise to any impressions, are obstructed in their operations, as when one is born blind or deaf; not only the impressions are lost, but also their correspondent ideas; so that there never appears in the mind, the least trace of either of them.

(1978:5)

Here what Hume is citing as evidence for the Copy Principle is the fact, which is a fact about human beings in general, that sensory limitations lead to limitations in thought – manifested in limitations in linguistic understanding. And, in general, unless we understand the Copy Principle as involving something like thesis (A) it is impossible to see how the evidence he cites for it is relevant.

Interpreting the Copy Principle in this way does not, of course, involve departing from Hume's understanding of it as an empirical truth. For (A) is still a *genetic* thesis about the past causes of present understanding. Nor, so far, have we arrived at any resolution of the puzzle of the missing shade of blue, for this is as much a counter-example to the Copy Principle interpreted as involving thesis (A) as it is to the Copy Principle not understood in this way.

However, a possible resolution of the puzzle may now be approached by noting that meaning empiricism need not take the form of a genetic thesis. What is at the heart of meaning empiricism is the thought that linguistic understanding must be connected *in some way* with experience, that is, that experience *in some way* sets limits to what is expressible in language. In Hume and Locke this thought takes the form of a genetic thesis which asserts that one can only express in language those features of the world of which *one has had* experience (or which one can construct out of those features of which one has had experience). But meaning empiricism need not be thought of in this way. An alternative non-genetic formulation would be that one can only express in language those features of the world which *are capable of being encountered in* experience. This is a weaker thesis than thesis (A) and does not take the form of a causal thesis, as thesis (A) does. And, most importantly for our present purposes, the case of the missing shade of blue is no counter-example to it. For, as Hume makes absolutely clear, the case as he imagines it simply involves that, as a matter of happy philosophical accident, a particular shade of blue, experienced by other people, is not experienced by one particular person who has experienced many other shades of blue. But there is no suggestion that the missing shade of blue is *unencounterable*. By contrast, Hume could not allow that an impression of substance or necessary connection in the world is simply something which has, as a matter of fact, not been encountered by someone, or anyone. Impressions corresponding to these concepts, Hume thinks, *are* impossible.

Thus, if we suppose that, at some level of his thought, Hume recognised that what really mattered to him was not the Copy Principle, as such, but merely the non-genetic form of empiricism which it entails, we can see why he should be so unperturbed by the case of the missing shade of blue, and should think his polemical deployment of the Copy Principle justified despite it. It is only the genetic *form* in which Hume, following Locke, phrases his empiricism, rather than its *content*, as such, to which the missing shade of blue is a counter-example.

This, then, is one suggestion about how the puzzle of Hume's insouciance concerning the missing shade of blue can be solved. I now turn to another, which again crucially involves the thought that what is really important to Hume is a weaker form of empiricism than that he officially espouses. (For a fuller exposition of this solution, see Fogelin 1992.)

The first point to be noted, in approaching this alternative solution is (as Fogelin expresses it) that there is a kind of atomism which Hume does *not* accept. According to this kind of atomism 'each simple impression [or simple idea] is a pure content standing in no systematic relationship to any other simple impression [or idea] except for being qualitatively identical with it or simply qualitatively different from it' (Fogelin 1992:72). Thus only complex impressions can bear relations of similarity or dissimilarity to one another which do not reduce simply to identity or difference. In particular, only complex impressions can resemble one another to various degrees (in virtue of sharing more or fewer parts).

Hume explicitly denies this view in the 'Appendix' to the *Treatise*:

'Tis evident that even different simple ideas may have similarity or resemblance to each other; nor is it necessary that the point or circumstance of resemblance shou'd be distinct and separable from that in which they differ. *Blue* and *green* are different simple ideas, but are more resembling than *blue* and *scarlet*; tho' their perfect simplicity excludes all possibility of separation or distinction. 'Tis the same case with particular sounds, and tastes and smells. These admit of infinite resemblances upon general appearance and comparison, without having any common circumstance the same.

And of this we may be certain, even from the very abstract terms *simple idea*. They comprehend all simple ideas under them. These resemble each other in their simplicity. And yet from their very nature, which excludes all composition, this circumstance, in which they resemble, is not distinguishable nor separable from the rest. 'Tis the same case with all the degrees in any quality. They are all resembling, and yet the quality, in any individual, is not distinct from the degree.

(1978:637)

It is because Hume thinks in this way of simple ideas and impressions that he is led to his example of the missing shade of blue. The various shades of blue, he thinks, although simple, can be arrayed in sequence with the most closely resembling shades being placed together. Then, in such a linear arrangement, if one shade of blue is missing there will be a noticeable gap – a place where two adjacent shades are noticeably less resembling than the other adjacent shades. In this circumstance, Hume thinks, the mind will be able to make for itself the simple idea out of the materials already presented to it.

This is thus very different from the situation Hume has in mind when he denies, immediately before introducing the example of the missing shade of blue, that the mind can raise up for itself 'a just idea' of the taste of a pineapple, without actually having tasted it (1978:5). Perhaps the mind could raise up this idea for itself if it were presented with a sequence of more and less resembling tastes, so arranged as to indicate, as in the case of the shades of blue, the absence of one particular taste. But Hume clearly does not have any such situation in mind when he mentions the taste of pineapple. Rather, he introduces the example simply to indicate that simple impressions of a particular sense may be unavailable to a perceiver not only when the organs of sensation are entirely lacking (the person is blind or deaf) but also when, as a matter of contingent fact, they have never been activated to produce a particular impression.

The shade of blue thus *is* a counter-example to the Copy Principle, just as Hume says. But, unlike the simple idea of the taste of a pineapple, produced in the circumstances Hume imagines, it is not a counter-example to a slightly weaker principle which can be stated as follows:

(B) Any simple idea is (1) a copy of a simple resembling impression or (2) an idea of the degree of a particular quality produced in the mind by the presentation thereto of simple impressions of contiguous degrees of the quality.

Although this principle is weaker than the Copy Principle and does not entail the empiricist maxim that there is nothing in the intellect which is not first in the senses, it still requires that all simple ideas must be preceded in the mind by simple impressions related to them in a certain way: it is just that the 'certain way' is no longer required to be exact resemblance. Moreover, the empiricist maxim, just stated, is anyway something Hume cannot accept because of the existence of complex ideas. Thus admitting the missing shade of blue as a counter-example to the original, strong version of the Copy Principle need not be seen as the blank and incomprehensible rejection of an otherwise unquestioned empiricism it might at first seem.

But the crucial question remains: can Hume's polemical use of the Copy Principle be understood if we take this weaker form of empiricism, represented by principle (B), to be the only form of it to which he is truly committed? It can. The philosophical concepts Hume attacks using the Copy Principle – concepts like substance and necessary connection in the world – are not concepts like that of the missing shade of blue. They are not concepts of degrees of a quality, to other degrees of which we can suppose ourselves to have been exposed. Perhaps it makes sense to speak of 'degrees of substantiality'. Perhaps some things are more truly substances than others. But the concept of substance is not itself the concept of a determinate degree of some determinable quality. The same is true of the concept of necessary connection.

Thus these concepts are on a par with the concept of the taste of a pineapple in the circumstance in which Hume supposes a simple idea of that quality has not been obtained. The exception to the Copy Principle provided by the missing shade of blue can thus be explained in a way that does not extend to these problematic philosophical concepts, and so Hume's confidence that the unqualified Copy Principle can be applied to them is justifiably undiminished by it.

The association of ideas

According to Hume, once ideas are derived from impressions, their occurrence in the mind exhibits regularities which can be reduced to three general patterns. These patterns – the principles of the association of ideas – account for the sequence in which thoughts pass through the mind; they account for the particular complex ideas we form from the simple ideas with which our minds are stocked and, finally, for the fact that 'languages so nearly correspond to each other, nature in a manner pointing out to every one those simple ideas, which are most proper to be united into a complex one' (1978:11). In outlining his associationism Hume takes for granted his imagistic theory of thought and this sometimes affects his formulation of the principles of association of ideas, but even if Hume's imagistic theory of thought is mistaken, his associationism might be correct, and vice versa.

The three principles of the association of ideas are: *resemblance*, *contiguity in time and place* and *cause and effect*.

The effect of resemblance he explains thus:

'Tis plain that in the course of our thinking, and in the constant revolution of our ideas, our imagination moves easily from one idea to any other that *resembles* it, and this quality alone is to the fancy a sufficient bond of association.

(1978:11)

Here we see an evident instance of the influence of Hume's theory of thought on his formulation of his associationism, but what he has in mind is plain enough and illustrated clearly elsewhere: the sight of a portrait, for example, will make us think of the person portrayed. The way in which Hume thinks contiguity operates is also clear. The thought of an object or event leads to thoughts of other things which have been encountered in its neighbourhood or other events that happened at the same time. Finally, the thought or perception of something tends to give rise to the thought of its cause or effect.

It might seem at first sight implausible that every transition in thought can be explained by appeal to just these three relations, and

Hume's sensitivity to this possible objection is shown by his stress on 'the full extent of these relations' (1978:11). Objects are connected together in the imagination, he says, not only where they are *immediately* resembling, contiguous or causally related, 'but also when there is interposed betwixt them a third object, which bears to both of them any of these relations. This may be carried on to a great length' (1978:11).

Hence Hume shows that it is not actually the three relations he specifies which are for him the principles of association of ideas, but rather, to use a modern technical term, their *ancestrals*: the relations linking any two things between which intermediates can be found linked by the three specified relations. Thus he is able to explain, in conformity to his theory of the association of ideas, how one's thought can pass from one cousin to another, and in general from one blood relation to another. For:

> cousins in the fourth degree are connected by causation, if I may be allowed to use that term; but not so closely as brothers, much less as child and parent. In general we may observe, that all relations of blood depend upon cause and effect.
>
> (1978:11–12)

Again he generalizes beyond his initial characterization of the principles of association by explaining that:

> Two objects may be consider'd as plac'd in [the] relation [of causation], as well when one is the cause of any of the actions or motions of the other, as when the former is the cause of the latter.
>
> (1978:12)

And:

> We may carry this farther, and remark, not only that two objects are connected by the relation of cause and effect, when the one produces a motion or any action in the other, but also when it has a power of producing it.
>
> (1978:12)

Thus, for example, Hume is now able to explain transitions of thought between ideas of master and servant, or of judge and convict, or between ideas of anyone in a position of power in society and a subordinate, as conforming to his principles of the association of ideas. And in general, he believes, by explaining 'the full extent' of the relations of resemblance, contiguity and causation in this way, he has set forth an empirical theory which is adequate to explain all transitions in thought and can serve as a theory of 'a kind of ATTRACTION, which in the mental world will be found to have as extraordinary effects as in the natural, and to shew itself in as many and as various forms' (1978:13).

Later in the *Treatise* Hume refers to the three principles of association as 'natural relations'. By this he means that they are relations by which the human mind is naturally affected, so that thought slides easily from one to another object when the objects are so related. Of course, there are other relations. The term Hume uses for relations in general is 'philosophical relations'. Thus for Hume any relation, distance for example, is a philosophical relation, but the only natural relations are resemblance, contiguity and causation (when 'the full extent of these relations' is understood). This, in a sentence, is Hume's theory of the association of ideas.

So far I have only mentioned one of the two roles that the principles of association have in Hume's theory of mind, that of accounting for transitions in thought. But they have an equally important role in explaining belief. The way this happens is as follows. When an idea occurs in the mind it will attract into the mind another idea of an object which is related to it by one of the three natural relations and, equally, when an impression occurs in the mind it will attract into the mind an idea which is related to it by one of the three natural relations. For impressions and ideas differ only in vivacity and not in content, and the natural relations hold between ideas in virtue of their contents. But when it is an *impression* that occurs in the mind it not only attracts related ideas into the mind, it also transfers to them a share of its vivacity, it *enlivens* the associated ideas. However, according to Hume, as we shall see, a belief can be nothing more than a lively and forceful idea. So if an idea is sufficiently enlivened it becomes a belief. Thus the principles of association, by serving as conduits through which vivacity can be transferred, provide Hume with an account of the origin of belief.

However, this account later provides him with a considerable problem with which he struggles in Section 10 of Part III. For Hume does *not* wish to allow that all three principles of association can serve equally well to explain belief, or at least belief in matter of fact. He maintains that only causation can do so. Thus he has to explain why the two relations of contiguity and resemblance, though indeed capable of serving as conduits through which vivacity can be transferred from impressions to ideas, can never serve as conduits of a sufficient quantity of vivacity to transform an idea into a belief, but can only strengthen an already formed belief. His solution to this problem, in brief, is that when it is the cause–effect link that attracts an idea into the mind there is just one (possibly complex) idea to be attracted into the mind (since causes are necessary and sufficient conditions of their effects). On the other hand, when resemblance or contiguity are functioning as natural relations, many different ideas will be apt to be pulled into the mind by the associative link, since any thing will resemble several others equally well, and any thing has many neighbours. Since this is so the vivacity transmitted in these latter cases is *shared out* among the related ideas so that each gets only a portion of the available vivacity, not enough to transform it into a belief. By contrast, when the cause–effect relation is serving as the natural relation, since 'the thought is always determined to pass from the impression to the idea, and from that particular impression to that particular idea without any choice or hesitation' (1978:110), all the vivacity accrues to a single idea.

We can see why Hume is so determined to deny that contiguity or resemblance to a present impression can account for the origin of belief, if we step outside the confines of his vocabulary for the moment and note that belief is a propositional attitude: a belief is a belief *that* something is the case, which may be true or false. This point creates no problem, at least no immediately evident problem, for Hume's thesis that causation can serve as a conduit through which sufficient vivacity can be transferred from impression to idea to transform an idea into a belief, since an inference to an effect, on observing its cause, or to a cause on observing its effect, is easily representable as the formation of a belief that a certain proposition is true. When I see the first billiard ball strike the second I immediately form the belief *that the second billiard ball will now move*. In general, when I observe an event of a type I know to cause a second type of event I immediately form the belief *that an event of the second type will now occur in the vicinity*.

But how could contiguity or resemblance serve in this way as the origin of belief?

Suppose I have seen Peter and Jane together in the past. Seeing Peter, am I supposed to form the belief *that Jane is in the vicinity?* I might do so if *whenever* (and only whenever) I see Peter I see Jane, but such constant conjunction is precisely, for Hume, what underpins our belief in a causal connection. Observed contiguity without constant conjunction could plainly have no such effect. Nor, of course, could contiguity explain the formation of any other belief about Jane – that she still exists, for example. Thus in resisting the view that contiguity can channel sufficient vivacity to an associated idea from an impression to transform it into an idea, Hume is showing himself (despite the mechanistic character of his explanation) to be sensitive to an evident fact, even though his theory of thought makes it difficult for him to state it clearly.

The same is true of his denial that resemblance can serve as a sufficient conduit for vivacity transference. In this case the point is more evident still, if possible. Suppose Peter and Jane are twins. So, in accordance with Hume's views, when I think of Peter I am apt to think of Jane and when I see Peter I am apt to think of Jane. What belief should I form when I see Peter? If neither causation nor contiguity is supposed to be operative I cannot form the belief *that Jane is in the vicinity*. But what other belief could I form? *That Jane is somewhere?* Our minds do not and could not work in these ways, and it is to Hume's great credit that he recognises the fact, despite the inconvenience it causes him.

Abstract ideas

It is not only the missing shade of blue which at first sight seems to be acknowledged by Hume to be a counter-example to the Copy

Principle. Hume says also that our idea of time 'is not derived from a particular impression mix'd up with others and plainly distinguishable from them' (1978:36) and the context makes it clear that he would say the same about our idea of space. The idea of existence is similarly said not to be 'derived from any particular impression' (1978:66). Yet Hume does not hesitate to employ the Copy Principle critically in the very sections in which these apparent counter-examples are retailed. Thus he denies the existence of ideas of a vacuum and of time without change because there are no impressions from which these ideas can be derived (1978:65). The explanation of the apparent inconsistency is straightforward, however. Hume thinks that the ideas of space, time and existence are genuine ones, albeit not derived from any *particular* impression separable from all others, because he thinks of them as *abstract* ideas. Whereas, he thinks, we cannot have even an abstract idea of time without change or of empty space.

To understand Hume's position better, then, we need to turn to his theory of abstract ideas, in which he sets himself to defend Berkeley's position against Locke's.

The notion of an abstract idea is a philosophical attempt to make sense of the generality of thought. We can think thoughts about *all men* – tall and short, fat and thin – and *all triangles* – isosceles, scalene and equilateral. To Locke, Berkeley and Hume it seemed that to account for such generality in thought we must posit ideas which are *general in their representation*. But how can an idea be general in its representation? How can our idea of man represent equally all men, fat and thin, tall or short? To do so, it seems, it must represent *all* possible human sizes or shapes or *no* particular sizes and shapes at all.

Locke takes the latter option. For him abstract ideas are the products of the process of abstraction, a process which involves separating what is in real existence inseparable to produce a sketchy indeterminate idea:

> [children] when time and a larger Acquaintance has made them observe, that there are a great many other things in the world that in some common agreements of shape, and several other qualities ... resemble their father and mother ... frame an *idea*, which they find many particulars do partake in, and to that they give ... the

name *man* ... And *thus they come to have a general name*, and a general *idea*. Wherein they make nothing new, but only leave out of the complex *idea* they had of *Peter* and *James*, *Mary* and *Jane*, that which is peculiar to each, and retain only what is common to them all.

(Essay III, iii.7)

Going further, Locke thinks, we can abstract away additional features and achieve the yet more abstract idea of *animal*:

which new idea is made not by any addition, but only as before by leaving out the shape, and some other properties signified by the name *man*, and retaining only a body, with life, sense, and spontaneous motion, comprehended under the name animal.

(Essay III, iii.8)

Berkeley flatly denies that such a process of abstraction is possible in Section 10 of the introduction to his *Principles of Human Knowledge*:

Whether others have this wonderful faculty of *abstracting their ideas*, they best can tell: for my self I find indeed I have a faculty of imagining or representing to my self the ideas of those particular things I have perceived and of variously compounding and dividing them. I can imagine a man with two heads or the upper part of a man joined to the body of a horse. I can consider the hand, the eye, the nose, each by it self abstracted from the rest of the body. But then whatever hand or eye I imagine, it must have some particular shape and colour. Likewise the idea of a man that I form to my self, must be of a white, or a black, or a tawny, or a straight, or a crooked, a tall or a low, or a middle sized man. I cannot by any effort of thought conceive the abstract idea above described [that is, one retaining only what is common to all men].

(1949:29)

Although this represents the impossibility of forming abstract ideas as a psychological fact, in reality what lies behind Berkeley's contention is rather the belief that such ideas are a logical impossibility. The reason for this is that they must be indeterminate: the abstract idea of a triangle, for example, must be neither equilateral nor not equilateral. But such indeterminate objects cannot exist.

Of course, it is natural to protest at this juncture that this objection rests on the absurd assumption that an idea of a triangle must itself *be* a triangle. But there are three points to be made in response to this. First, arguably, Berkeley did make this assumption. Second, Locke himself writes as if the assumption is correct, for example, in the notorious passage in which (to Berkeley's glee) he refers to 'the general idea of a triangle, [which] must be neither Oblique, nor Rectangle, neither Equilateral, Equicrural, nor Scalenon: but all and none of these at once' (*Essay* IV, vii.9). Third, and most importantly for our purposes, *Hume* certainly takes it for granted that an idea of a triangle must be triangular – as we have seen, *his* reification of ideas is absolutely self-conscious and so, as Hume sees it, the admission of Lockean abstract ideas necessarily involves an admission that reality itself can be indeterminate, which is a possibility he rejects out of hand.

Hume begins his discussion of abstract ideas by affirming what he takes to be Berkeley's view, that 'all general ideas are nothing but particular ones, annexed to a certain term, which gives them a more extensive signification, and makes them recall upon occasion other individuals which are similar to them' (1978:17). He then declares that he will endeavour to confirm it by some arguments which will put it beyond controversy.

Hume sees the argument for what he takes to be the Lockean position to rest upon a plain dilemma:

> The abstract idea of a man represents men of all sizes and all qualities; which 'tis concluded it cannot do, but either by representing at once all possible sizes and all possible qualities, or by representing no particular one at all.

> (1978:18)

But, it seems, the first alternative is impossible since, it seems, it requires an infinite capacity in the mind, so we are left with the second, Lockean, alternative. Yet Hume argues that this involves something 'utterly impossible' – 'to conceive any quantity or quality without forming a precise notion of its degree' (1978:18) – and that the first alternative is not impossible after all, since even though the capacity of the mind is not infinite 'we can at once form a notion of all possible degrees of quantity and quality, in such a manner, at least, as, however imperfect, may serve all the purposes of reflexion and conversation' (1978:18).

Hume gives three arguments against the Lockean alternative.

The first begins with a statement of his Separability Principle and its 'inverse' (what we would call the converse):

that whatever objects are different are distinguishable and that whatever objects are distinguishable are separable by the thought and imagination. And we may here add, that these propositions are equally true in the *inverse*, and that whatever objects are separable are also distinguishable, and that whatever objects are distinguishable are also different.

(1978:18)

Given these principles, Hume argues, the separability of a precise degree of a quality or quantity from that quantity or quality itself, which is implied by Lockean abstraction, is impossible. He takes the relation of the precise length of a line to the line itself as his illustration of the relation between a precise degree of a quantity and the quantity itself and argues thus:

'tis evident at first sight that the precise length of a line is not different nor distinguishable from the line itself; nor the precise degree of any quantity from the quantity. These ideas, therefore, admit no more of separation than they do of distinction and difference. They are consequently conjoined with each other in the conception; and the general idea of a line, not withstanding all our abstractions and refinements has in its appearance in the mind a precise degree of quantity and quality; however it may be made to represent others, which have different degrees of length.

(1978:18)

The argument here is that since the length of a line *is* the line itself, by the inverse of the Separability Principle it cannot be distinguishable or separable from the line itself (nothing is separable from itself). So, in so far as Lockean abstraction implies such separation, it is impossible. Because the length of a line *is* the line, the idea of the length of the line *is* the idea of the line and no sketchy or indeterminate idea of a Lockean kind can possibly be found. And the same holds generally for the precise degree of any quantity and that quantity; they are inseparable because they are identical.

What is interesting about this argument is its starting point. Hume simply takes it as evident that the precise length of a line *is* the line itself, that the relation between them is identity. But why should this be accepted? Do we not, in general, distinguish between individuals and their qualities, lines and their lengths, bodies and their shapes, objects and their actions, and is this distinction not all that is required by an opponent of Hume?

The answer to this question is that we do indeed, in our ordinary thought and talk, make this distinction, and many philosophers accept it as a genuine feature of the world, but Hume does not. In fact, he explicitly asserts, in the case of each of the three instances just cited (1978:12, 18, 25) the identity of the items we commonly distinguish, and given his principles he must do so. To see why this is so we must recall that he accepts not just the Separability Principle but also the Conceivability Principle:

> Whatever is clearly conceived may exist, and whatever is clearly conceived after any manner, may exist after the same manner.
>
> (1978:233)

These principles are put to use in his crucial argument against the traditional notion of substance as 'something which may exist by itself' that 'this definition agrees to everything that can possibly be conceived; and never will serve to distinguish substance from accident or the soul from its perceptions'. Hume explains:

> For thus I reason. Whatever is clearly conceiv'd may exist, and whatever is clearly conceiv'd after any manner, may exist after the same

manner. This is one principle, which has been already acknowledged. Again, everything which is different, is distinguishable and everything which is distinguishable is separable by the imagination. This is another principle. My conclusion from both is, that since all our perceptions are different from each other, and from everything else in the universe they are also distinct and separable, and may be considered as separately existent, and may exist separately, and have no need of anything else to support their existence. They are, therefore, substances, as far as this definition explains a substance.

(1978:233)

This argument (as we shall see later) is the linchpin in Hume's rejection of a substantial self, distinct from perceptions, and his espousal of the bundle theory of the self. But its present importance is that it enables us to see why Hume is so confident that the precise length of a line cannot be distinguished from the line, or the degree of any quantity from the quantity. For, on Hume's principles, there are *no* dependent entities. If the length of a line is an object distinct from the line it can exist separately from that line, or any line, and has no need of anything else to support its existence. Similarly, if the shape of a body is an object distinct from the body, it can exist separately from it, and if the action of an object is distinct from the object it can exist separately. In general, if qualities are distinct from things they can exist separately from them – like the Cheshire Cat's grin. But this Hume thinks is absurd, and this is the basis of his first argument against Lockean abstraction.

Hume's second argument against Lockean abstract ideas appeals again to one of his fundamental principles, the Copy Principle:

all our simple ideas in their first appearance are deriv'd from simple impressions, which are correspondent to them, and which they exactly represent.

(1978:4)

This principle enables him to make a transition from what he takes to be a logical truth about impressions to a corresponding conclusion about ideas.

The logical truth about impressions, to deny which (Hume claims) includes 'the flattest of all contradictions, *viz* that it is possible for the same thing both to be and not be' (1978:19), is:

> that no object can appear to the senses; or in other words, that no impression can become present to the mind, without being determined in its degrees both of quantity and quality.
>
> (1978:19)

To appreciate Hume's confidence that he has here hit upon a logical truth, it is important to recall the point that impressions for Hume are not representations of other (external) things, as even ideas of sensation are for Locke; and they are themselves (the only) possessors of both primary and secondary qualities. Thus, to deny the determinateness of impressions, for Hume, is to acknowledge indeterminacy *in the world*. But, if the indeterminateness of impressions is a logical absurdity, the same (Hume argues) must be true of that of ideas. For ideas and impressions differ only in degree of vivacity and the conclusion that the indeterminacy of impressions is a logical absurdity was 'not founded upon any particular degree of vivacity' (1978:19).

Hume's third argument against Lockean abstract ideas again moves from the impossibility of indeterminacy in the world to the impossibility of indeterminacy in thought, this time via an appeal to the Conceivability Principle.

Since indeterminate objects are impossible we can form no idea of an indeterminate object, otherwise (by the Conceivability Principle) they would be possible. But 'to form the idea of an object, and to form an idea simply is the same thing; the reference of the idea to an object being an extraneous denomination of which in itself it bears no mark or character' (1978:20). Any idea can count as an idea representing an object, in the only sense Hume allows, in virtue of its resemblance to that object (that is, that impression). So, if ideas indeterminate in their own character were possible they would serve as ideas *of* indeterminate objects. But it has already been established that such ideas are impossible. Thus, abstract ideas are, therefore, in themselves, individual, however, they may become general in their representation. The image in the mind is only that of a particular object, tho' the application of it in our reasoning be the same, as if it were universal.

(1978:20)

Thus we see how Hume's rejection of Lockean abstract ideas is not an incidental element in his philosophy, but derives from assumptions and principles which are fundamental to it: the Copy Principle and the insistence that the *only* difference between impressions and ideas is one of degrees of vivacity; the Separability Principle, and consequent rejection of any dependent entities and the reification of perceptions; the Conceivability Principle and the denial of any distinction between an idea's resembling an object or impression and its representing, or being an idea *of*, that object or impression.

Having rejected Locke's account of how general thoughts are possible, however, Hume now needs to provide his own. He does so by proposing an account which he takes to be an elaboration of Berkeley's. The key to understanding general thought, he suggests, is to suppose that it is secondary to the use of general terms. For Locke, words become general by being associated with general or abstract ideas; for Hume, ideas become general or abstract by being associated with general terms. Nothing that goes on in the mind of thinkers that is describable without reference to language can make their thought to be general rather than particular. Rather, we apply ideas beyond their nature, that is, beyond their determinateness and particularity and come to think general thoughts in the following way.

When we have found a resemblance among several objects, notwithstanding their differences, we apply the same name to all of them. Then, after acquiring a custom of this kind,

the hearing of that name revives the idea of one of these objects ... But as the same word is supposed to have been frequently applied to other individuals ... the word not being able to revive the idea of all these individuals only touches the soul ... and revives that custom, which we have acquired by surveying them. They are not really and in fact present to the mind, but only in power; nor do we

> draw them all out distinctly in the imagination, but keep ourselves
> in a readiness to survey any of them, as we may be prompted by a
> present design or necessity. The word raises up an individual idea,
> along with a certain custom, and that custom produces any other
> individual one, for which we may have occasion.
>
> (1978:20–1)

Thus, according to Hume it is possible for a particular idea to acquire
a general representation by being associated with a term with which is
also associated a custom, or disposition, to produce other particular
ideas of resembling objects as need be. What makes the idea general,
however, is nothing in its intrinsic character, but only the custom with
which it is linked via the general term.

Of course, for this to be a complete account of how general
thought is possible Hume needs to say more about the crucial custom
or disposition. He does say more, but not enough. What he emphasizes is that it is part of the custom to produce ideas of
counter-examples to false generalizations whenever one encounters
them, even if the particular idea in one's mind when the generalization
is first uttered is one which conforms to it:

> Thus should we mention the word triangle, and form the idea of a
> particular equilateral one to correspond to it, and should we after-
> wards assert, *that the three angles of a triangle are equal to each
> other*, the other individuals of a scalenum and isosceles, which are
> overlooked at first, immediately crowd in upon us, and make us
> perceive the falsehood of this proposition, though it be true with
> relation to that idea, which we had formed.
>
> (1978:21)

This does not always happen, as Hume admits, but he gives no explanation of *when* it does not happen save that in such a case there is
'some imperfection in [the mind's] faculties' (1978:21).

But Hume's main point is that however, in more detail, the custom
he describes is to be characterized, it is this alone that can account for
general thought. In fact, he admits, the *same* particular idea may
occur in the minds of people who are thinking *different* general

thoughts. The idea of an equilateral triangle, for example, may be present before the mind of a man who is thinking of equilateral triangles, one who is thinking of triangles generally and one who is thinking of all regular figures. The difference between the thoughts will consist in no *actual* difference but in the different dispositions of the three thinkers, their different states of readiness to produce, as need be, ideas of resembling objects. And indeed, even if *no* idea is before the mind, such a state of readiness may be present and will suffice for thought:

> we do not annex distinct and complete ideas to every term we make use of
>
> (1978:23)

> ... it being usual, after the frequent use of terms ... to omit the idea, which we wou'd express by them, and to preserve only the custom by which we recal the idea at pleasure.
>
> (1978:224)

Hume ends his section on abstract ideas by declaring that he will employ 'the same principles' (as already outlined) 'to explain that *distinction of reason* which is so much talked of, and is so little understood, in the schools' (1978:24) (that is, the 'scholastic' tradition which arose in the medieval universities and is associated with the methods and theses of the major philosophers of the thirteenth and fourteenth centuries, Aquinas, Scotus and Ockham; 'distinctions of reason' are also discussed by Descartes in *Principles of Philosophy* 1.60, where they are contrasted with the 'real distinction' which, Descartes maintained, held between mind and body). Commentators have found what he goes on to say puzzling and hard to reconcile with other elements of his philosophy. But with the foregoing in mind, as we shall see, his discussion is easily understood.

Hume begins by giving examples of what is meant by a 'distinction of reason': the distinction between figure and body figured and between motion and body moved. Another example he goes on to discuss is that between the colour and form of a body. Recalling the exposition of Hume's first argument against Lockean abstract ideas will make it evident that Hume cannot recognise these distinctions as genuine ones: the figure of a body cannot be a distinct object from the body. Otherwise, Hume supposes, by the Separability Principle it could exist separately and independently of the existence of any body. The same reasoning applies to the other pairs of putatively distinct items. In Hume's view there can no more be a real distinction here than in the case of a line and its length. As he puts it himself:

> The difficulty of explaining this distinction arises from the principle above explained, *that all ideas which are different are separable*. For it follows from thence, that if the figure be different from the body their ideas must be separable as well as distinguishable: if they be not different, their ideas can neither be separable nor distinguishable. What then is meant by a distinction of reason, since it implies neither a difference nor separation?
>
> (1978:25)

Thus 'distinctions of reason' are an important topic for Hume because as construed 'in the schools' they are distinctions between inseparable entities and thus counter-examples to the Separability Principle. He therefore needs an alternative account of them which is consistent with his own principles.

At this point Hume introduces his own positive account of abstract ideas, which he is entitled to do since, although his argument against Lockean abstract ideas uses the Separability Principle, his positive account does not. Put simply his position is that the ideas connected with the terms 'the figure of body X' and 'body X' are abstract ideas. That is to say, there need be *no* actual difference between someone who is thinking of body X and someone who is thinking of the figure of body X; the same particular determinate idea may be before the minds of the two thinkers. But the man who is thinking of the figure of body X will be in a different state of readiness from a man who is thinking of body X itself. The man who is thinking of the figure of body X will be disposed to produce ideas of other bodies, resembling body X in respect of shape; whereas the man who is thinking of body X will not be so disposed, but rather will be disposed to produce ideas of body X itself, differing in respect of shape but otherwise the same.

Thus, Hume thinks, his account of abstract ideas enables him to explain what 'distinctions of reason' are. They are not distinctions actually present in thought (for any idea which can serve as the abstract idea of a figure will be a particular idea which can equally well serve as the abstract idea of a body). They are, rather, distinctions only made possible through language, and the general thought which language makes possible.

Hume's theory of thought

It was said earlier in this chapter that Hume, like Locke, endorsed an imagistic theory of thought, which (particularly in virtue of the work of Wittgenstein) can now be recognised to be untenable, since any image can be interpreted in more than one way and so no image can determine the identity of what is being thought.

However, in the light of Hume's discussion of abstract ideas we can now see that Hume's theory is more complex and insightful than at first appears. Hume can endorse Wittgenstein's famous remark: 'If God had looked into my mind he would not have seen there, of whom I was thinking' (1968:217). He can agree that nothing that goes on at a time can constitute a thought with a particular content; that, in fact, whatever happens in my consciousness when I think a thought places no constraint on the content of my thought; and indeed that no image at all is necessary for me to think a particular thought.

Nevertheless, the Wittgensteinian critique of the imagistic account of thinking still applies to Hume, even when his theory of abstract ideas is taken into account. For Wittgenstein's main point – that an idea (something whose identity is constituted by what is the case at the time it is before the mind) cannot in itself compel the understanding to take it in one way rather than another – applies equally to any *finite* set of items of like character (and, indeed, to any infinite set, though the vulnerability of Hume's position to the Wittgensteinian critique does not depend on this extension). So Hume's account of what makes my thought to be a thought of a triangle rather than an equilateral triangle or any regular figure when I have before my mind an idea, for example, of an equilateral triangle – namely, that I stand in readiness to recall other particular ideas to mind – cannot explain the determinateness of my thought unless the set of images I associate with the word 'triangle' – and which I stand in readiness to recall – is the set of all *possible* triangle images. But to interpret Hume's account in this way is to rob it of all possible empirical import. The theory can pretend to be explanatory only if the associated images are ones which we stand in readiness to *recall* because they are ones we have previously *encountered* – otherwise the notion of 'recall' has lost any empirical meaning.

To illustrate the difficulty, consider Wittgenstein's famous example of the incapacity of images to determine their own interpretation:

> I see a picture: it represents an old man walking up a steep path leaning on a stick. How? Might it not have looked just the same if he had been sliding downhill in that position? Perhaps a Martian would describe the picture so.
>
> (1968:54)

In other words, we still need an account of what it is to take a picture one way or the other. The intrinsic qualities of the picture do not determine this. But no (finite) addition of signs or extra features to the picture will determine a unique interpretation. If we add arrows, for example, to indicate the direction of movement they too can be interpreted in different ways. (Maybe the Martians fire their arrows feathered end first.) Whatever we add will just be another sign in as much need of interpretation as the original. And the same will be true if we add a set of resembling images of men walking up hills. Each such image can be interpreted in more than one way and the whole set taken together can be interpreted in more than one way.

If the image before the mind, then, is one of the mountain scene Wittgenstein describes, it is not determined thereby that I am thinking of 'an old man walking up a hill' – if God were to look into my mind and see that image he would not be able to deduce from its presence that that was the content of my thought. And if somehow a whole (finite) array of resembling images were simultaneously *actually* present, the situation would not be any different. Nor then can it be any different if only one image is actually before my mind and the remainder there only 'in power', as Hume puts it.

Thus Hume's theory of thought, despite the Wittgensteinian insights contained in his account of abstract ideas, fails to explain, in the face of the Wittgensteinian challenge, how determinate thought is possible. This is a failing, however, shared by every theory of thought which has so far been produced. And the challenge must remain unanswered until it is shown how thought (and other intentional states) can at the same time both sustain normative relations to what is external to them and be available to their subjects as occurrent phenomena of consciousness, whose identity is constituted by what is the case at the time of their occurrence – it is this task which Wittgenstein's 'rule-following considerations' (1968) have left to his successors.

Further reading

Material particularly relevant to the themes of this chapter is contained in:

Bennett, J. (1971) *Locke, Berkeley and Hume*, Oxford: Clarendon Press.

Berkeley, G. (1949) *The Works of George Berkeley*, vol.2, ed. A.A. Luce and T.E. Jessop, London: Thomas Nelson & Sons.

Fogelin, R. (1992) *Philosophical Interpretations*, Oxford: Oxford University Press.

Locke, J. (1961) *An Essay Concerning Human Understanding*, ed. J. Yolton, London: Dent.

Norton, D.F. (ed.) (1993) *The Cambridge Companion to Hume*, Cambridge: Cambridge University Press.

Wittgenstein, L. (1968) *Philosophical Investigations*, trans. G.E.M. Anscombe, Oxford: Blackwell.

Yolton, J. (1970) *Locke and the Compass of Human Understanding*, Cambridge: Cambridge University Press.

Chapter 3

Causation, induction and necessary connection

The grounds of belief and the role of causation

In Part III of the *Treatise*, entitled 'Of Knowledge and Probability', Hume's discussion is largely devoted to two questions:

1   What assures us of 'existences and objects we do not see or feel' (1978:74)? In other words, what leads us to form beliefs about unobserved matters of fact: that the sun will rise tomorrow, that Africa still exists, that the Normans won the Battle of Hastings?
2   What is the correct account of causation? What does it mean to say that one thing causes another?

The connection between these two questions, he thinks, is that the only relation 'that can be trac'd beyond our senses and informs us of existences and objects, which we do not see or feel, is *causation*' (1978:74). That is, the answer to question (1) is 'causal inference'.

If this is correct then it is perfectly proper for Hume, given that he is interested in the foundation of belief in 'matters of fact' (an expression, in fact, used mainly in the first *Enquiry* rather than in the *Treatise*), or of belief in 'existences and objects we do not see or feel', to seek an analysis of the nature of causation. But is all matter-of-fact belief based on causation?

Evidently there are many beliefs I have, and think I am perfectly entitled to have, which by no stretch of the imagination can be thought of as ones resulting from causal inference. I believe that all bachelors are unmarried, for example. But this belief is not a result of causal inference. Again, I believe, but not on the basis of causal inference, that $2 + 2 = 4$, that the angles of a triangle sum to 180° and that if snow is white and grass is green then snow is white. That is, in general, beliefs based wholly on knowledge of meanings, beliefs about mathematical facts and beliefs about logical truths are manifestly not the product of causal inference in the way in which this is true of beliefs about what will happen if you get shot/take arsenic/drop the hammer on your toe.

But Hume takes for granted a distinction between beliefs of the first type just listed and those for which he wishes to maintain his thesis. This distinction is set out in the first two sections of Part III of the *Treatise*: Section 1, 'Of Knowledge', and Section 2, 'Of Probability and of the Idea of Cause and Effect'. It is the distinction between, on the one hand, propositions based on *relations of ideas* and, on the other hand, propositions not so based, but based rather on relations which 'may be chang'd without any change in the ideas' (1978:69), the latter being propositions neatly referred to in the *Enquiry* as ones concerning 'matters of fact and existence'. Propositions of the first type listed above then all turn out to be propositions based on relations of ideas.

The details of Hume's discussion of this distinction in the *Treatise* are difficult and confused (see Bennett 1971: Chapter 10 for elaboration). In places he clearly has in mind a distinction between those relations between objects which *supervene* on their non-relational qualities, in the sense that they cannot alter without any alteration in their non-relational qualities and obtain in virtue of their non-relational qualities, and those which do not. Thus the non-supervening relations of *contiguity* and *distance* are cited as relations which 'may be changed merely by an alteration of their place, without any change on the objects themselves or on their ideas' (1978:69), and contrasted with the supervening relations of *resemblance* and *proportions in quantity or number*. However, this is not the distinction which is really of concern to him. Rather, his basic idea can be understood if we remember that ideas, for Hume, are the materials of thought (that is, concepts) and double up as meanings. (Plausibly the distinction between supervenient and non-supervenient relations intrudes because ideas are also copies of impressions, impressions are appearances of objects, and how an object appears depends on its non-relational qualities.)

Given that ideas are meanings, a proposition 'based on relations of ideas' is one that can be seen to be true by reflecting on the meanings of the words used to express it. 'All bachelors are unmarried men' is a paradigm example of this type of proposition – an *analytic* proposition as it is now known – and Hume's position can now be stated as the claim that all the types of proposition listed three paragraphs above are analytic propositions. Of course, it is certainly not the case that all such propositions are *obviously* true, like 'All bachelors are unmarried'. A complicated arithmetical identity, for example, may be true but require many pages of proof; it certainly cannot be thought of as obviously true. But nonetheless, Hume will say, if it *is* true at all, it will be true merely in virtue of 'relations of ideas', it will be analytic and discoverable as true by reflection on meanings.

To defend this position Hume needs and makes, again borrowing from Locke (*Essay* IV, ii.1), a distinction between *intuition* and *demonstration* (1978:70). An analytic truth like 'All bachelors are unmarried' can be seen to be true immediately by anyone who understands what it means: its truth is accessible to intuition. Not so for a complicated or even moderately complicated mathematical theorem. But even in such a case, Hume believes, if we write down the proof of the theorem then (1) the starting point, and (2) each link to the next thought, will be intuitively evident in just the way 'All bachelors are unmarried' is. Hence, by going through the proof, it will be possible to see how the theorem, even though not obviously true, is true merely in virtue of relations of ideas. And Hume believes that all beliefs of the type listed above are knowable either by intuition or demonstration.

According to Hume such propositions also have several other features:

1   They can be known to be true by thought alone, that is, without having to check whether they are true in experience. That is, Hume regards them as a priori knowable.

2   They are necessary and not contingent truths, and so not vulnerable to refutation. It seems fairly obvious that if a proposition is true in virtue of its meaning then it must state what could not be otherwise (since the only way a sentence used to express it could be used to say something false would be to change its meaning). But the converse is not obvious. Perhaps there are necessary truths which are not analytic and not a priori as, in fact, many recent philosophers – following Kripke (1980) – would claim. Examples of such putative necessary a posteriori truths include ones stating the properties of natural kinds – that water is H_2O, that gold is an element – and those stating the origins of particular objects – that I originated from a particular sperm and ovum, or that the table I am now writing on was originally made from a particular piece of wood. (The argument for their necessity which Kripke gives turns on considerations of identity: if, for example, this table was originally made from a particular piece of wood, he claims, then we can see that *no* table, however alike, made from different wood, could have been *this very table*, and so it must be necessarily true of this table that it had the material origin it in fact had.) Prima facie such propositions, if they are indeed necessary a posteriori truths, provide a rich fund of counter-examples to Hume's denial of necessary connections between distinct existences. Indeed, Hume's claim that there are no necessary connections between distinct existences is precisely the claim that if X and Y are distinct existences then either could exist in a universe from which the other was absent – which is flatly incompatible with Kripke's thesis of the essentiality of origin since I and my father, for example, are certainly distinct existences, but according to Kripke I could never have existed if my father had not.

3   Finally, Hume regards propositions based on relations of ideas as the only ones which are, strictly speaking, *knowable*. Propositions concerning matters of fact and existence, he says, are not knowable but only probable. In this he again follows Locke and is using terminology in a way that was standard for his time. To our ears the position sounds unduly sceptical but there is no substantive scepticism involved. And, in fact, Hume, more than Locke, is aware of the air of oddity in this way of drawing the distinction and acknowledges it: 'One would appear ridiculous, who wou'd say that 'tis only probable the sun will rise tomorrow, or that all men must die, tho' 'tis plain we have no further assurance of these facts, than what experience affords us' (1978:124). In consequence he revises his terminology and distinguishes between *proofs* and probabilities. But he still insists that a fundamental distinction remains between propositions concerning matters of fact – however certain we may be of them – and propositions expressing relations of ideas. That is, even if someone is, as a matter of psychological fact, as certain that the sun will rise tomorrow, as he is that $1 + 1 = 2$, the difference between the two propositions will still remain that the first cannot be seen to be true by perceiving relations between ideas, and the second can.

The distinction is expressed most eloquently in Hume's own words, in the following passage from the first *Enquiry*:

All the objects of human reason and enquiry may be divided into two kinds, to wit, *Relations of Ideas* and *Matters of Fact*. Of the first kind are the sciences of Geometry, Algebra and Arithmetic; and, in short, every affirmation which is either intuitively or demonstratively certain. ... Propositions of this kind are discoverable by the mere operation of thought, without dependence on what is anywhere existent in the universe ... Matters of fact ... are not ascertained in the same manner; nor is our evidence of their truth, however great, of a like nature ... The contrary of every matter of fact is still possible; because it can never imply a contradiction and is conceived by the mind with the same facility and distinctness, as if ever so conformable to reality ... Were it demonstratively false, it would imply a contradiction and could never be distinctly perceived by the mind.

(1975:25–6)

The idea of cause

By distinguishing propositions based on relations of ideas from propositions concerning matters of fact and existence, Hume is thus able to specify more exactly the focus of his contention that causation is the only relation that 'can be trac'd beyond our senses, and informs us of the existences and objects, which we do not see or feel' (1978:74).

Two other relations he considers as possible candidates for this role are *identity* and *situation in time and place*, which he describes as relations which 'depend not on the idea' (1978:73), meaning (here quite clearly) relations which do not supervene on the non-relational qualities of the related objects. We have already noted the way in which this is true of contiguity and distance, which are what Hume has in mind in talking of situations in time and place: one cannot deduce anything about the spatio-temporal relations of objects from descriptions, however detailed, of their non-relational properties. The same, Hume maintains, holds of identity: the fact that an object I perceive now is exactly like one I saw earlier is not proof that it is numerically the same. (In addition, the fact that an object I see now is different from one I saw earlier is no proof that it is numerically distinct, though this is not a point Hume notes or would accept.) However, Hume claims, these relations, unlike causation, are not able to produce such

a connexion, as to give us assurance from the existence or action of one object, that 'twas followed or preceded by any other existence or action; nor can the other two relations ever be made use of in reasoning, except so far as they either affect or are affected by [causation].

(1978:74)

As to situation in time and place, Hume says:

There is nothing in any objects to persuade us that they are either always *remote* or always *contiguous*; and when from experience and observation we discover, that their relation in this particular is invariable, we always conclude that there is some secret *cause*, which separates or unites them.

(1978: 74)

An illustration of Hume's point might be helpful. If, as I am walking down the street, I notice two people passing close to one another, one walking away from me and one towards me, say, I will not, just on that basis, form the expectation that these people will be found always or frequently together in the future; but if I do subsequently see them together on many occasions, I will conclude that there is some cause to explain the fact – they are friends, or work at the same place, or catch the same bus every morning, or whatever. Conversely, if I observe two of my colleagues, say, standing at opposite ends of a seminar room and not talking I will not, just on that basis, infer that they will never be found together; but if I frequently observe their separation, in situations in which contiguity would be equally likely, I will conclude that there is some cause at work – perhaps they have quarrelled, for example.

As to identity:

We readily suppose an object may continue individually the same, tho' several times absent from and present to the senses; and ascribe to it an identity, notwithstanding the interruption of the perception, whenever we conclude that if we had kept our eye or hand constantly upon it, it wou'd have conveyed an invariable and uninterrupted perception. But this conclusion beyond the impressions of our senses can be founded only on the connexion of *cause and effect*; nor can we otherwise have any security, that the object is not changed upon us, however much the new object may resemble that which was formerly present to the senses. Whenever we discover such a perfect resemblance, we consider, whether it be common in that species of objects; whether possibly or probably any cause could operate in producing the change and resemblance;

and according as we determine concerning these causes and effects, we form our judgement concerning the identity of the object.

(1978:74)

Again Hume's point is worth illustrating. If I observe men who look exactly alike on two successive days I will conclude that very likely they are one and the same man, since a perfect resemblance is not 'common in that species of objects'. On the other hand, there is 'nothing so like as eggs' (Hume 1975:36), so I do not conclude, on the basis of their exact resemblance, that the egg I see on my breakfast plate today is the very one which I had for breakfast yesterday, miraculously reconstituted. Again, if I see today someone who looks exactly like a schoolfriend of thirty years ago, I will not infer, on account of that resemblance, that he is that very person; on the contrary, the resemblance will rather convince me that he is *not*, because of the changes which inevitably accompany ageing in human beings. On the other hand, if I find myself lost in the Himalayas, thirty years after my first visit, and see a mountain looking exactly like one I saw thirty years ago, I *will* infer that very probably it is the same mountain, since in this 'species of objects' thirty years makes no discernible change.

Thus what Hume says in the quoted passage seems unexceptionable, and a clear and accurate (if very abbreviated) description of the factors which do, in fact, influence our judgements of identity and distinctness over time. However, as we shall see later, matters are not so straightforward for Hume. The reasoning process he so accurately describes here is one in which the existence of the external world is *assumed*. But when Hume turns to the question of the grounds for our belief in the external world or matter (or rather, as he puts it, setting aside as irrelevant to his enquiry any issue of justification, the question of the *causes* of our belief 'in body'), it turns out to be an essential element of his answer that we are caused to make judgements of identity over time simply by the presence in our experience of what he calls 'constancy', that is, exact similarity between later and earlier perceptions, and that these judgements in turn operate to produce a belief in an unperceived external world. Hume thinks this mechanism of belief formation is a function of the imagination, in the narrow and disreputable sense of that term distinguished earlier, in which it is opposed both to demonstrative and to causal reasoning, which he makes explicit in Section 9 of Part III (1978:117). Nevertheless, it is one by which we are led, otherwise than by causal inference, to a belief in objects we do not see or feel. It is a large question, to which we shall return later in this chapter, whether Hume will be able to distinguish (except by mere stipulation) this process of belief formation from that involving causal inference, in a way which will allow him to maintain that identity is never 'made use of in *reasoning* except so far as it is affected by [causation]' (1978:74; my emphasis).

For the present, however, with Hume, we can move on. Having argued to his own satisfaction that causal inference is the only reasoning process which can lead us to existences and objects not seen or felt, without more ado Hume now proceeds to his second question: what is the correct analysis of the idea of causation?

Hume approaches this question, as he must, given his Copy Principle, by looking for an impression or impressions from which the idea can be derived. In the first place he notes that no *quality* of the things we call causes or effects can be the origin of our idea of causation, for we cannot discover any single quality common to them all:

> indeed there is nothing existent, either externally or internally, which is not to be consider'd either as a cause or an effect; tho' 'tis plain there is no one quality, which universally belongs to all beings and gives them a title to that denomination.
>
> (1978:75)

Hume concludes: 'The idea, then, of causation must be derived from some *relation* among objects; and that relation we must now endeavour to discover' (1978:75).

Hume finds three distinct and separable relations to be involved in causation:

1   *Contiguity.* Hume does not claim that the things which we consider to be causes and effects are always immediately contiguous – that is, adjacent in time and space – for there may be a chain of causes between A (the cause) and Z (the effect). But in

this case, Hume says, we will suppose a sequence of immediately contiguous items between A and Z – that is, we will rule out action at a distance. Thus, he says, at least according to the popular opinion, contiguity is essential to causation. However, he indicates that this is merely a provisional assessment 'till we can find a more proper occasion to clear up this matter' (1978:75). A footnote at this point refers us to Part IV, Section 5, where Hume reveals the basis of his caution. This is his contention that '*an object may exist and yet be nowhere*: and, I assert, that this is not only possible, but that the greatest part of beings do and must exist after this manner' (1978:235). He goes on to explain:

> A moral reflection cannot be placed on the right or on the left hand of a passion; nor can a smell or sound be either of a circular or of a square figure. These objects and perceptions, so far from requiring any particular place are absolutely incompatible with it.
>
> (1978:236)

Spatial contiguity at least, then, is not essential to causation since 'the greatest part of beings' are incapable of it. But that Hume does not trouble to make the matter clear at this point is merely indicative of his lack of interest in contiguity. It is, he thinks, *an* element (when suitably qualified) in our idea of causation, but one whose origin is unproblematic.

2   *Priority in time*. Again Hume spends little time on this notion. He notes that there is some controversy whether causes must precede effects and gives an argument that this must be so. But he sums up his discussion of priority in time by saying:

> If this argument appear satisfactory 'tis well. If not I beg the reader to allow me the same liberty which I have used in the preceding case [of contiguity], of supposing it such. For he shall find that the affair is of no great importance.
>
> (1978:76)

This is so, Hume thinks, because the idea of priority in time, like that of contiguity, is an unproblematic one – its origin in our experience is clear; so either it is *not* an element in our idea of causation and therefore does not pose a problem for the analysis of that idea, or it *is* an element, and still does not pose a problem.

3   *Necessary connection.* Hume regards this relation as of much more importance than the other two elements in the idea of causation, and not just as a third necessary but insufficient element on a par with the others. The explanation of this is obvious if we keep in mind that Hume's interest in causation derives from his desire to explain the nature of the *inferences* we make from facts given to us in observation to unobserved facts. Now Hume has already argued that:

> we ought not to receive as reasoning any of the observations we may make concerning ... the relations of *time* and *place*; since in none of them the mind can go beyond what is immediately present to the senses, either to discover the real existence or the relations of objects.
>
> (1978:73)

Since causation *does* enable the mind to go beyond the senses, then, it cannot do so in virtue of its containing as components contiguity and priority in time, which are relations of time and place, but must rather do so in virtue of its third component, necessary connection. And a necessary connection is obviously, at first sight, a candidate for grounding such an inference. For given a *perception* of an object of a certain type and a *perception* of a necessary connection between it and another type of object, it would seem that a basis would thereby be provided in perception for an inference from the existence of the perceived object to the existence of another, unperceived, object of the second type.

But now Hume confronts a difficulty. The perception of necessary connection *would* ground inference if it were present. But, Hume claims, he *cannot find* any impression of necessary connection, in any case of what is usually regarded as a cause–effect link, from which the idea of necessary connection may be derived. When we observe what happens in such a case, Hume claims, we perceive the known *qualities* of the objects we think of as cause and effect (their colours and shapes and sizes, for example) 'but the relation of cause and effect depends not in the least on *them*' (1978:77), and we perceive spatio-temporal relations (contiguity and succession) 'which I have already regarded as imperfect and unsatisfactory' (1978:77), but that is all – we do not perceive any necessary connection. If, to take Hume's favourite example of billiards, we watch while the white cue-ball strikes a red ball and the latter moves off, all we actually perceive, Hume insists, is a change in spatio-temporal relations. There is nothing observable present to which the name 'necessary connection' can be applied, and this is so whatever example of causation we take.

Hume does not at this point explain the basis of his confidence in this negative contention, though this becomes clearer later at the beginning of Section 6. However, it is worth reflecting on what it would be like to observe necessary connection given the role Hume ascribes to it as the ground of inference. We can observe priority in time and contiguity in time and space when *two* suitably related objects are presented to us, but, of course, in this circumstance (as Hume writes) 'we call *this* perception rather than reasoning; nor is there in this case any exercise of the thought, or any action, properly speaking, but a mere passive admission of the impressions thro' the organs of sensation' (1978:73). If inference is to take place only *one* of the objects can be present to sense. But then the relation (of priority in time or contiguity) will *not* be present. Necessary connection, if it is to play the role Hume ascribes to it, must be capable of being presented to sense when both the connected objects are also presented *and* when only one of them is presented, so that inference to the second is possible. In this respect it must be unlike the relations of contiguity and priority in time, and indeed unlike *any* other relation. Hume's puzzlement as to how there could be such a thing in the world to be observed may now seem somewhat more understandable.

What matters for now, however, is that Hume does not take his failure to find an impression of necessary connection as a proof that there can be exceptions to the principle of the priority of impressions to ideas: 'This would be too strong a proof of levity and inconstancy' (1978:77). Instead he embarks on an extended search for the impression of necessary connection, suggesting that his procedure must be like those

> in search of any thing that lies conceal'd from them, and not finding it in the place they expected, beat about all the neighbouring fields, without any certain view or design, in hopes their good fortune will at last guide them to what they search for.
>
> (1978:78)

Thus he turns from the direct survey of the question of the nature of necessary connection and takes up instead the two questions: (1) 'For what reason we pronounce it *necessary* that every thing whose existence has a beginning, shou'd also have a cause', and (2) 'why we conclude that such particular causes must *necessarily* have such particular effects, and what is the nature of that inference we draw from the one to the other, and of the belief we repose in it' (1978:78). He takes up the first question in Section 3 and the second, after some preliminaries, in Section 6. The course of his discussion is complicated and takes some unexpected turns, but it must be remembered that all along his aim is the same: to find the impression of necessary connection from which the idea of necessary connection must be derived. He never doubts that there *is* such an impression and of course, despite his arch reference to his enquiry being 'without any certain view or design' and merely 'in hopes' that 'good fortune will at last guide him' to what he seeks (1978:78), in the end he finds it, though in a place he clearly believes will come as a great surprise to his reader.

The Causal Maxim

Hume's first question (why do we believe it necessary that every beginning of existence should have a cause?) is the question why we believe what he calls the 'general maxim in philosophy, that *whatever begins to exist, must have a cause of existence*' (1978:78) – hereafter 'the Causal Maxim'. This is the proposition that it is a *necessary truth* that every beginning of existence has a cause. Thus Hume's first question is distinct from his second question (why do we think that such particular causes must necessarily have such particular effects?), as one can see most easily by observing that it could be a necessary truth that every beginning of existence had a cause even if particular causes were not necessarily connected to particular effects, and particular causes could be necessarily connected to particular effects even if it were not a necessary truth that all beginnings of existence had a cause.

Despite the difference between Hume's two questions he nonetheless thinks that the same answer will serve for both (1978:82). The reason for this is that he thinks that the one answer to both questions that can be ruled out straightaway is that we think these things because they are *true* and that we can *see*, by rational reflection, that they are true. In fact, Hume thinks, there is *no* necessity that every beginning of existence have a cause and no necessary connection between particular causes and effects. The explanation of our believing otherwise is merely a psychological compulsion, which, Hume thinks, explains both beliefs (though he only elaborates its operation in the case of the second). In fact, when Hume discusses the Causal Maxim he does not even attempt to explain why we believe it. Instead he devotes the whole of Section 3 (i) to arguing that it is not a necessary truth that every beginning of existence has a cause and (ii) to offering refutations of several purported demonstrations that it *is* a necessary truth.

The first part of Hume's discussion in Section 3 appeals to the divide already drawn between propositions concerning relations of ideas and the rest. If it is a necessary truth, Hume argues, that every beginning of existence has a cause, it must be either intuitively certain or demonstrable. But it is not intuitively certain: it is not *obviously* contradictory to deny it. Nor, however, is it demonstratively certain: its denial is not a statement of an impossibility, not even one that can only be exposed by a complicated chain of reasoning. Hume attempts to prove his point by an argument from imagination:

as all distinct ideas are separable from each other, and as the ideas of cause and effect are evidently distinct, 'twill be easy for us to conceive any object to be non-existent this moment, and existent the next, without conjoining to it the distinct idea of a cause or productive principle. The separation, therefore, of the idea of a cause from that of a beginning of existence, is plainly possible for the imagination; and consequently the actual separation of these objects is so far possible, that it implies no contradiction nor absurdity; and is therefore incapable of being refuted by any reasoning from mere ideas; without which 'tis impossible to demonstrate the necessity of a cause.

(1978:79–80)

This argument (like Hume's first argument against Lockean abstract ideas) and his later argument (quoted in the previous chapter) for the applicability of the notion of 'a substance' to 'everything that can possibly be conceiv'd' and, in particular, to all perceptions (1978:233) appeals to the combination of the Separability Principle and the Conceivability Principle. The argument is that a cause is a distinct object from its effect. So it is distinguishable and separable by the imagination. Consequently the actual separation of the objects is possible and that object which is, in fact, the effect (the 'beginning of existence') may exist without need of *any* cause.

In fact, not only does Hume's argument at this point appeal to the same principles as his argument for the universal applicability of the notion of substance, it is, in fact, merely a special case of that argument. For the latter argument, as we saw, can be construed as an argument that *there are no dependent entities*, but if beginnings of existence were to require causes they *would* be dependent entities and so Hume must maintain that they do not.

Seeing the argument against the Causal Maxim and the argument for the universal applicability of the notion of substance as related in this way, enables us to see also that Hume's argument against the Causal Maxim (and *mutatis mutandis*, of course, his argument about substance) is fallacious.

Hume states the conclusion of the argument about substance (as applied to perceptions) to be that 'all our perceptions are different from each other, and from everything else in the universe ... and have no need of anything else to support their existence' (1978:233) and earlier he argues that perceptions are capable of existing unperceived by any mind as follows:

> we may observe that what we call a *mind*, is nothing but a heap or collection of different perceptions ... Now as every perception may ... be consider'd as separably existent ... it evidently follows, that there is no absurdity in separating any particular perception from the mind.
>
> (1978:207)

However, even given Hume's conception of the mind and granted the correctness of the Separability and Conceivability Principles, this last argument fails. For suppose a perception P might have existed outside of the bundles of perceptions with which it is, in fact, combined; it does not follow that P might have existed outside of *any* more comprehensive bundle of perceptions – outside of *any* mind. Again, looking now at the argument for the substantiality of all perceptions, given the Separability and Conceivability Principles, Hume can conclude that any perception P can exist in the absence of any other distinct perception P1 and indeed in the absence of any other distinct object X, but it does not follow that P has 'no need of anything else' to support its existence – in the sense that P might have been the whole universe. For it is compatible with the argument that *in order for P to exist something else must exist* even if *there is no particular thing which must exist if P exists*.

This reasoning can now be applied to Hume's argument against the Causal Maxim. Given the Separability and Conceivability Principles any object X, whose coming into existence is the effect of a particular cause C, might have come into existence in the absence of C. But it does not follow that X might have come into existence without *any* cause. For it is compatible with the argument that *in order for X to exist some cause must bring it into existence* even if *there is no particular cause which must bring X into existence if X is brought into existence*.

To see more clearly the consistency of these two forms of proposition consider a concrete case. One can imagine water in a pot boiling without any heat under it. Thus it is plausible to say that one can know what it would be like to establish the occurrence of *this* phenomenon without *this* cause. And since heat is the *actual* cause of boiling water this provides support for the proposition *that there is no particular cause which must be the one which brings about the boiling of water*. But I cannot imagine, in any similar way, water boiling without *any* cause, and I cannot imagine what positive experience would count in favour of such a discovery. Thus no positive experience I can imagine provides support for the proposition *that water may boil without any cause at all*. Thus the former of these italicized propositions does not entail the latter and so is consistent with its negation, namely, that *in order for the water to boil some cause or other of its boiling must be present*. Thus Hume's first argument against the Causal Maxim actually moves his case forward not at all. But, of course, if the Causal Maxim is a truth then the necessity of a cause to any beginning of existence must be demonstrable. In the second part of Section 3 Hume therefore examines four purported demonstrations and argues that in each case it fails. The first purported demonstration, which Hume ascribes in a footnote to Hobbes, is the most interesting but also the most obscure. As Hume reports it, Hobbes' argument is:

All the points of time and place ... in which we can suppose any object to begin to exist, are in themselves equal; and unless there be some cause, which is peculiar to one time and to one place, and which by that means determines and fixes the existence, it must remain in eternal suspence; and the object can never begin to be, for want of something to fix its beginning.

(1978:80)

Hume replies:

But I ask; Is there any more difficulty in supposing the time and place to be fixed without a cause than to suppose the existence to be determined in that manner? The first question that occurs on this subject is always, *whether* the object shall exist or not. The next *when* and *where* it shall begin to exist. If the removal of a cause be

> intuitively absurd in the one case, it must be so in the other: And if
> that absurdity be not clear without a proof in the one case, it will
> equally require one in the other.

(1978:80)

It would take us far too long to go into the complexities of this debate. A fascinating discussion of it is contained in G.E.M. Anscombe's British Academy Lecture 'Times, Beginnings and Causes' (included in Anscombe 1981) which tracks down the relevant passage in Hobbes. I will only suggest here (for the detailed argument, see Anscombe) that Hobbes' argument does seem to establish *something* that Hume might have wished to deny, namely, that we could have no positive reason in our experience for describing a situation as 'a beginning of existence of a substance (a thing)' unless we also had positive reason to describe it as one in which a particular cause was present. For example, our experience could not warrant us in describing a situation as one in which a rabbit *came into existence* (rather than *travelled* here from elsewhere in some other form, as a gaseous cloud or electro-magnetic radiation or whatever) unless it also warranted us in ascribing its existence to a particular cause. But this does not entail the logical impossibility of a beginning of existence without a cause – certainly not if we take the notion of 'a beginning of existence' widely enough to cover events which are not the origins of substances (as Hume does), and even if we think only of the origins of substances, the *logical impossibility* of such an occurrence does not follow.

The second argument for the Causal Maxim, ascribed to Samuel Clarke (the English rationalist philosopher and theologian and champion of Newton), Hume states as follows:

> Every thing ... must have a cause; for if any thing wanted a cause, it
> wou'd produce itself, that is, exist before it existed, which is impossible.

(1978:80)

Hume's reply hits the nail on the head: to say that something comes into existence without a cause is *not* to imply that it is its own cause;

on the contrary, it is incompatible with the claim that it is its own cause. Hence, whatever absurdities there may be in the idea of self-causation they do not provide any reason for denying the possibility of uncaused events. In Hume's words:

> This reasoning is plainly unconclusive because it supposes that in our denial of a cause we still grant ... that there must be a cause ... But to say that any thing comes into existence without a cause is not to affirm that 'tis its own cause; but on the contrary, in excluding all external causes [one] excludes *a fortiori* the thing itself, which is created.
>
> (1978: 80–1)

The third argument, ascribed to Locke, Hume states as follows:

> Whatever is produc'd without any cause ... has *nothing* for its cause. But nothing can never be a cause, no more than it can be something, or equal to two right angles ... Consequently ... every object has a real cause of its existence.
>
> (1978:81)

Hume's reply to this argument is essentially the same as his reply to the previous argument: it begs the question from the outset by assuming what it sets out to prove, namely, that every event has a cause. In this case the question is begged by assuming that if an event does not have an 'ordinary' cause, as one may put it, it must have an 'extraordinary' cause – '*nothing*'. But if it really has no cause then it has *no* cause, not an 'extraordinary' cause. (Of course, if something has no cause it will be *true*, using the word 'nothing' in its ordinary grammar, that nothing is its cause. But the argument misconstrues the grammar of 'nothing' to arrive at its conclusion and Hume, in his criticism, assumes the misconstrual to be correct – presumably for the sake of argument.)

After presenting these arguments Hume briefly considers a fourth argument for the Causal Maxim, not ascribed to any author, which he deems more frivolous still, namely, that every event must have a cause because every *effect* must have a cause. He notes that one might as well argue that every man must be married because every husband must have a wife.

Hume then sums up: he takes himself to have shown that there can be no intuitive or demonstrative knowledge that every event has a cause, and hence that belief in the Causal Maxim must necessarily arise, not from reason, but from experience – which leads us astray (because it is not a *necessary* truth that every event has a cause; it is important to note that Hume never questions that it is in fact true). The next question he says is this: how can experience give rise to such a principle? And this question he now proposes to sink into the second question he earlier identified as a possible line on to the impression of necessary connection (which, remember, it is still the whole object of the exercise to find): why do we conclude that such particular causes must necessarily have such particular effects and why do we form an inference from one to the other? This is our next topic.

Inference from the observed to the unobserved

After some preliminary material in Sections 4 and 5, Hume moves to the crucial part of his discussion in Section 6; at this point it will be useful to have before us a brief overview of the general shape of his ensuing argument.

First, Hume argues in Section 6 that observation of any single event, if we consider it *by itself*, will never provide us with any basis for belief that some other specific type of event will follow. Hence, he argues, *past experience* is necessary to provide the foundation for causal inference. But we can have no *reason* to expect the future to resemble the past, since any argument for this general principle will necessarily be circular. Consequently, Hume concludes, just as it is not reason which convinces us of the truth of the Causal Maxim, so it is not reason which convinces us that there are necessary connections between particular causes and particular effects in virtue of which we are entitled to infer the effect on observing the cause:

> When the mind, therefore, passes from the idea or impression of one object to the idea or belief of another, it is not determined by reason, but by certain principles, which associate together the ideas

of these objects, and unite them in the imagination.

(1978:92)

Having argued all this, Hume at last (in Section 14) returns to the question which initiated his enquiry: how do we come by the idea of necessary connection? His answer is that since there is no necessary connection *between the objects which are causes and effects*, no necessity 'in the world' as we might briefly say, the *ideas* of the cause and effect must be simply bound together *in our minds* as a result of our past experience. Hence necessity is something that exists only in our minds, not in the objects themselves. Thus it is only in the mind that the impression of necessary connection is to be found, where it occurs as an accompaniment to our causal inferences. And it is from this impression that we derive the idea of necessity which is at the heart of our idea of causation.

With this brief overview in mind we can now return to the starting point of Hume's argument, which is the contention, in the first paragraph of Section 6 that 'there is no object, which implies the existence of any other if we consider these objects in themselves and never look beyond the ideas which we form of them' (1978:86–7). It is his conviction of the correctness of this claim which underlies his confidence that we can get no impression of necessary connection from the objects: the objects are *not* necessarily connected, so there is nothing suitable between them for there to be an impression of. This contention is thus a crucial one for Hume, despite the briskness of his statement of it, and in making it he is putting himself against a massive philosophical tradition to be found on both sides of the empiricist/rationalist divide.

We have already noted, in Chapter 1, Malebranche's definition of a 'true cause': one such that the mind perceives a necessary connection between it and its effect. In Spinoza we find the following (Axiom 3, Book I of the *Ethics*):

From a given determinate cause an effect necessarily follows; and, on the other hand, if no determinate cause be given it is impossible that an effect can follow.

(Spinoza 1949:42)

And in Chapter 9 of Hobbes' *Elements of Philosophy Concerning Body*:

> a CAUSE simply, or *an entire cause is the aggregate of all the accidents both of the agents how many so ever they be, and of the patients, put together, which when they are supposed to be present, it cannot be understood but that the effect is produced at the same instant; and if any one of them be absent it cannot be understood but that the effect is not produced.*

> (1994:121)

The idea, expressed most explicitly in this last passage, that a cause–effect link must be something *which can be understood*, rather than something which must just be accepted as a brute fact, is what Hume is most fundamentally opposed to. One way in which this idea can surface in a philosopher's writings, as we have seen, is in the contention that causes and effects are necessarily connected. But another expression of the same idea is that causes and effects must have something in common, some likeness or common feature which allows us to see how they can be linked. Thus Descartes in the *Third Meditation*:

> Now it is manifest by the natural light of nature that there must be at least as much reality in the efficient and total cause as in the effect of that cause. For where, I ask, would the effect get its reality from, if not the cause? And how could the cause give it to the effect unless it possessed it?

> (1984:28)

This principle underlies Descartes' first argument for the existence of God, and Locke argues similarly:

> whatsoever is first of all things must necessarily contain in it and actually have, at least, all the perfections that can ever after exist; nor can it ever give to another any perfection that it hath not, either actually in itself or at least in a higher degree: it necessarily follows that the first eternal being cannot be matter.

Again Locke writes, in the same paragraph:

> [It is] as impossible to conceive that ever bare incogitative matter should produce a thinking intelligent being, as that nothing should of itself produce matter.
>
> (*Essay* IV, x.8)

And also:

> It is evident, that what had its being and beginning from another, must also have all that which is in and belongs to it from another too. All the powers it has must be owing to and received from the same source. This eternal source, then, of all being, must be the source and origin of all power; and so this eternal being must also be the most powerful.
>
> (*Essay* IV, x.4)

Hume's other chief empiricist predecessor, Berkeley, similarly argues that causes and effects must have something in common. It is an 'old known axiom', he thinks, that:

> nothing can give to another that which it hath not itself.
>
> (1949:236n.)

And so he is easily able to conclude:

> That a being endowed with knowledge and will, should produce or exhibit ideas is easily understood. But that a being which is utterly destitute of these faculties should be able to produce ideas, or in any sort to affect an intelligence, this I can never understand.
>
> (1949:242)

Against this, Hume's position is that 'any thing may produce any thing' (1978:173). Causation is never more than a brute fact. It is only through experience that we can learn what causes operate in the world:

> There are no objects which by the mere survey, without consulting experience, we can determine to be the causes of any other, and no objects which we can certainly determine in the same manner not to be the causes.
>
> (1978:173)

Thus, as Hume puts it in the 'Abstract':

> Were a man such as *Adam* created in the full vigour of understanding, without experience, he would never be able to infer motion in the second ball from the motion and impulse of the first. It is not anything that reason sees in the cause, which makes us infer the effect.
>
> (1978:650)

Hume takes himself to have established all this in the first paragraph of Section 6. Causes and effects are distinct events and thus, by the conjunction of the Separability and Conceivability Principles, either might occur in the absence of the other. Of course, there will be many different descriptions of the cause and many different descriptions of the effect, and propositions asserting the occurrence of the cause under some descriptions will entail propositions asserting the existence of the effect under some descriptions (for example, if the cause is X and the effect is Y, the occurrence of X under the description 'the cause of Y' will, trivially, entail the existence of the effect under the description 'Y'). But Hume is not making a claim about *propositional* entailments. His claim is that the very *object* which is the cause might have existed in a world in which the very *object* which is the effect did not exist, and conversely. As we have seen above, this is a contention that puts Hume at odds with proponents of Kripke's essentialism about the necessity of origin. It is tempting, perhaps, to attempt to read Hume in a way that does not involve this confrontation by interpreting him as saying that, under certain 'intrinsic' or 'non-relational' descriptions, causes and effects are not necessarily connected. But that way lies the road to trivialization (for how else is an 'intrinsic description' of something to be understood save as one entailing nothing about any distinct object?).

We should take Hume at his word: his contention, to which the arguments advanced by Kripke do indeed pose a major challenge, is that the *objects themselves* which are causes and effects are not necessarily connected.

Hume now moves on to the next stage of his argument:

'Tis ... by experience only that we can infer the existence of one object from that of another. The nature of [the] experience is this. We remember to have had frequent instances of the existence of one species of objects; and also remember, that the individuals of another species of objects have always attended them, and have existed in a regular order of contiguity and succession with regard to them. Thus we remember to have seen that species of object we call *flame* and to have felt that species of sensation we call *heat*. We likewise call to mind their constant conjunction in all past instances. Without any farther ceremony, we call the one *cause* and the other *effect*, and infer the existence of the one from that of the other.

(1978: 87)

So, according to Hume, we infer B's from A's and pronounce A's the cause of B's when we have experienced A's as constantly conjoined with B's. Thus he says:

We have insensibly discovered a new relation betwixt cause and effect, when we least expected it and were entirely employed upon another subject. This relation is their CONSTANT CONJUNCTION.

(1978:87)

However, as Hume immediately goes on to point out, it is not clear how this can constitute progress. For his aim is still, recall, to find the *impression* of necessary connection which is the *origin* of the *idea* of necessary connection essential to our idea of causation. But if this is not discernible between a single pair of objects related as cause and effect then equally it cannot be discernible between any *exactly resembling* pairs – otherwise they would not be exactly resembling:

> From the mere repetition of any past impression, even to infinity, there never will arise any new original idea, such as that of necessary connexion.
>
> (1978:88)

At this point, however, Hume drops a hint that the discovery of constant conjunction will after all lead him to his goal:

> having found, that after the discovery of the constant conjunction of any objects we always draw an inference from one object to another, we shall now examine the nature of that inference, and of the transition from the impression to the idea. Perhaps 'twill appear in the end that the necessary connexion depends on the inference, instead of the inference's depending on the necessary connexion.
>
> (1978:88)

The next few paragraphs, in which Hume 'examines the nature of that inference' contain his most famous argument, traditionally interpreted as Hume's 'sceptical condemnation of induction' – an argument that when we infer the existence of an unobserved effect from an observed cause (or vice versa), on the basis of experience of the constant conjunction of such events, our conclusion is necessarily unwarranted, our belief unreasonable, our mode of inference unjustifiable. An eloquent exposition of this interpretation of Hume's argument as an expression of 'scepticism about induction' is contained in Stroud's *Hume*. Stroud writes:

> [Hume] rejects 'reason' or 'the understanding' as the source of such [causal] inferences on the grounds that none of them are ever reasonable or rationally justifiable. This is his most famous sceptical result ... Past and present experience gives us ... no reason at all to believe anything about the unobserved ... [Hume] condemns as unjustifiable a whole mode of inference or pattern of reasoning

… Hume claims that [a] man [who uses past experience of constant conjunction as a basis for inferences to the unobserved] has no reason *to* believe what he does. His belief has no rational support or justification … As far as the competition for degrees of reasonableness is concerned, all possible beliefs about the unobserved are tied for last place.

(1977:52–4)

Another philosopher who reads Hume in this way is D.C. Stove (1973), who interprets Hume's 'inductive scepticism' as the claim that inductive arguments can never increase the probability of their conclusions. Stove interprets Hume as arriving at this sceptical conclusion from the thesis of *inductive fallibilism* – that no inductive argument can render its conclusion certain – via *deductivism* – the assumption that only deductively valid arguments, whose conclusions are entailed by their premises, can raise the probability of their conclusions, or (as it is sometimes put) that all arguments are either deductive or defective.

Other interpreters react against this sceptical interpretation of Hume. All he is arguing, they claim, is that if 'reason' is interpreted in a narrow, rationalistic way, which conforms to the deductivist assumption, then reason has nothing to do with our formation of beliefs about unobserved effects or causes on the basis of observed causes and effects (see Broughton 1983; Beauchamp and Rosenberg 1981). But if so, they suggest that he thought, so much the worse for the deductivist conception of reason. And if it is said that the conclusion – that our beliefs about unobserved matters of fact cannot be arrived at via deduction from beliefs about observed matters of fact – is too obvious to be interesting, the reply is that its obviousness is due to a philosophical climate of opinion created by Hume's argument itself. So, as Flew expresses it in his book *Hume's Philosophy of Belief*, to make this a criticism of Hume is to act 'rather in the spirit of the man who criticised *Hamlet* for being so full of quotations' (1961:73).

Let us now turn to Hume's text to see if this issue of interpretation can be resolved. Hume begins his examination of the nature of causal inference by asking:

Whether experience produces the idea by means of the understanding or of the imagination; whether we are determined by
reason to make the transition, or by a certain association and relation of perceptions.

(1978:88–9)

He states his conclusion by answering this question:

When the mind, therefore, passes from the idea or impression of
one object to the idea or belief of another it is not determined by
reason, but by certain principles which associate together the ideas
of these objects and unite them in the imagination.

(1978:92)

That reason is not what determines the mind's activity, Hume
thinks, can be established as follows: if reason did determine us, 'it
wou'd proceed upon' the principle (usually referred to as the
Uniformity Principle) that

instances of which we have had no experience, must resemble those of
which we have had experience, and that the course of nature
continues always uniformly the same.

(1978:89)

But there can be no *demonstrative* arguments for the Uniformity
Principle, whilst *probable* arguments for the Uniformity Principle
must run into a circle since:

probability is founded on the presumption of a resemblance
betwixt those objects, of which we have had experience, and those
of which we have had none; and therefore 'tis impossible this
presumption can arise from probability. The same principle cannot
be both the cause and effect of another.

(1978:90)

Since the Uniformity Principle cannot be established without circularity, and if reason determines us it must proceed upon it, it follows that reason does not determine us.

Thus the argument, largely in Hume's own words. But what does it mean?

A way of interpreting it, which stays close to the text, but neither reads the traditional radical scepticism about induction into Hume, nor reads him as attacking only a narrowly rationalistic sense of reason, is to take the causal language occurring in his argument literally. This literalist interpretation is suggested by Cannon (1979), Broughton (1983) (who, however, unnecessarily as I think, also reads 'reason' in Hume's discussion in a narrow rationalistic sense) and Garrett (1997). It is also implicit in Loeb (1991, 1995a, 1995b).

As Hume explains, we engage in the practice of inductive inference, of making inferences from observed events, via beliefs about causes and effects based on past experience, to beliefs about unobserved events. Do we do so *because* we accept an argument to the effect that such a practice is in some sense a desirable one to engage in? That is, is our engaging in the practice of inductive inference itself the *effect* of our accepting an argument that it is desirable to do so? On the proposed literalist interpretation, this is the meaning of Hume's question 'Does reason determine us?'. 'Determine' in the question has the meaning of 'cause'. Hume's argument is now that we can be determined by reason, in this sense, only if we infer that it is desirable to engage in inductive inference from (a set of premisses including) the Uniformity Principle, the principle that the future will resemble the past. This is the meaning of the claim that 'if reason determin'd us it would proceed upon that principle' (1978:89). That is, if our practice of inductive inference is the *effect* of our accepting an argument that it is desirable to do so, a premiss of that argument must be the Uniformity Principle, for no argument which did not have the Uniformity Principle as a premiss could have that effect on us.

However, Hume thinks, our accepting such an argument could be the cause of our engaging in the practice of inductive inference only if we had a basis for the Uniformity Principle in the form of an argument of which it was the conclusion. We could not be caused to engage in the practice of inductive inference by our acceptance of an argument, a premiss of which was the Uniformity Principle, unless we also had available an argument *for* the Uniformity Principle (for we could not believe the Uniformity Principle, antecedently to acquiring a disposition to engage in inductive inference, except on the basis of argument). But we could not have available a *demonstrative* argument for the Uniformity Principle, since there is no contradiction in denying that the future will be like the past: 'we can at least conceive a change in the course of nature' (1978:89). The argument for this is just a reapplication of the argument, given previously, that no contradiction can be found in the occurrence of a cause without its customary effect or vice versa, since as distinct events, by the conjunction of the Separability and Conceivability Principles, either can exist without the other. All Hume is doing, in denying that the Uniformity Principle can be demonstrated, is generalizing this to the claim that *any sequence* of past events is distinct from, and hence can occur in the absence of, any future event.

So if there is to be an argument for the Uniformity Principle it cannot be a demonstrative one. All that remains, however, is the possibility of a probable argument, an argument which involves inference from observed events to unobserved events via beliefs about causes and effects based on past experience.

Now we can indeed accept the Uniformity Principle on the basis of such an argument. We can argue:

In the past, the future has resembled the past.

Therefore, in the future, the future will resemble the past.

But we will only be prepared to reason in this way if we are already disposed to engage in the practice of inductive inference. Part of the *cause* of our accepting the Uniformity Principle if we argue thus will, therefore, be our disposition to engage in inductive inference.

However, in that case our acceptance of the Uniformity Principle as the result of so reasoning cannot be the *cause* of our being disposed to engage in the practice of inductive inference. For 'the same principle cannot be both the cause and effect of another' (1978:90). It cannot therefore be reason (that is, our acceptance either of a demonstrative or a probable, causal, argument) that determines – causes – us to engage in the practice of inductive inference. Rather it must be merely 'a certain association and relation of perceptions' (1978:89).

On this literalist interpretation 'reason' does not have to be understood in a narrow rationalistic sense, on which it is effectively restricted to what Hume calls 'demonstrative reasoning', to make sense of Hume's argument. Hence the fact that Hume argues at length that our acceptance of the Uniformity Principle cannot be based on probable reasoning (if 'reason' is to determine the mind's activity) is easily understood. For those interpreters who take Hume's argument to be using 'reason' in the narrow way, however, its complexity is an embarrassment; for it would seem that, so interpreted, all Hume needs to establish is that there can be no *demonstrative* arguments for the Uniformity Principle.

Perhaps the most compelling piece of textual evidence for this literalist interpretation of Hume's discussion is to be found, however, not in the *Treatise* itself, but in the corresponding section of the first *Enquiry* (Section 4 (ii)), in Hume's summary of the purpose of his argument. Unless we think that his purpose was quite different in the *Enquiry* than it was in the *Treatise*, or that he woefully misunderstood the nature of his own argument in the former work, or that he was being wholly dishonest with his reader, the evidence is, in fact, quite conclusive. Hume writes:

It is certain that the most ignorant peasants – nay infants, nay even brute beasts – improve by experience, and learn the qualities of natural objects, by observing the effects which result from them. When a child has felt the sensation of pain from touching the flame of a candle, he will be careful not to put his head near any candle; but will expect a similar effect from a cause which is similar in its sensible qualities and appearance. If you assert, therefore, that the understanding of the child is led into this conclusion by any process of argument or ratiocination, I may justly require you to produce that argument; nor have you any pretence to refuse so equitable a demand. You cannot say that the argument is abstruse, and may possibly escape your enquiry; since you confess that it is obvious to the capacity of the merest infant. If you hesitate, therefore, a moment, or, if, after reflection, you produce any intricate or profound argument, you, in a manner, give up the question, and confess that it is not reasoning which engages us to suppose the past resembling the future, and to expect similar effects from causes which are, to appearances, similar. This is the proposition which I intended to enforce in the present section. If I be right, I pretend not to have made any mighty discovery. And if I be wrong, I must acknowledge myself to be indeed a very backward scholar; since I cannot now discover an argument which, it seems, was perfectly familiar to me long before I was out of my cradle.

(1975:39)

However, even if we set this aside, there are in fact many passages in the *Treatise* itself which support the literalist interpretation. In particular, it has no difficulty in making sense of the many passages, both in Section 6 and subsequently, in which Hume does not hesitate to write as if causal inference is indeed a process of reasoning, and as if its products are products of reason. On the literalist interpretation this is exactly right. Our engagement in the practice of inductive inferences is not itself a product of reason, but any particular belief resulting from causal inference is a product of reason, since once we have acquired the disposition to expect similar effects from causes which are similar and, conversely, our exercise of that disposition in inductive inference (which Hume describes as 'reasoning') is a process whose causal upshot is a belief about the unobserved.

A further point in favour of the literalist interpretation is that it has no difficulty in making sense of the many passages in which Hume writes as if causal inference is justified or rational, and distinguishes it as being so from various modes of belief formation which he compares unfavourably to it. These passages have been particularly emphasized by Broughton (1983) and by Loeb (1991, 1995a, 1995b). Already, in the very paragraph in which Hume draws the conclusion that ''tis impossible this presumption [the Uniformity Principle] can arise from probability' (1978:90), he describes cause and effect as the 'only connexion or relation of objects ... on which we can found a just inference from one object to another' (1978:89). Again in Section 7 of Part III, on the same page on which he writes in the text 'when we pass from the impression of one [object] to the idea or belief of another, we are not determined by reason', we find in a footnote: 'We infer a cause immediately from its effect; and this inference is not only a true species of reasoning, but the strongest of all others' (1978:97).

In Section 9, as already noted, Hume attempts to distinguish the effects of cause and effect from the effects of resemblance and contiguity, which he does not wish to allow as belief-forming mechanisms. In doing so he distinguishes two systems of relations: one constituted by present impressions and ideas or impressions of memory, and a second, wider system constituted by ideas connected to the first system by custom, or the relation of cause and effect. He ascribes the first system to the memory and the senses, and the second to judgement. He goes on:

'tis this latter principle which peoples the world, and brings us acquaintance with such existences, as by their removal in time and place, lie beyond the reach of the senses and memory ... I form an idea of ROME, which I neither see nor remember, but which is connected with such impressions as I remember to have received from the conversation and books of travellers and historians. This idea of Rome I place in a certain situation on the idea of an object, which I call the globe ... I look backward and consider its first foundation; its several revolutions, successes and misfortunes. All this, and everything else, which I believe, are nothing but ideas; tho' by their force and settled order, arising from custom and the relation of cause and effect, they distinguish themselves from the other ideas, which are merely the offspring of the imagination.

(1978:108)

The distinction made here between 'judgement' and (mere) 'imagination' emerges again nine pages on in Hume's discussion of the effects on us of mere repetition, which he sardonically calls 'education':

I am persuaded, that upon examination we shall find more than half of those opinions, that prevail among mankind, to be owing to education, and that the principles, which are thus implicitly embrac'd, over-ballance, those, which are owing either to abstract reasoning or experience. As liars, by the frequent repetition of their lies, come at last to remember them; so the judgement, or rather the imagination, by the like means, may have ideas so strongly imprinted on it, and conceive them in so full a light, that they may operate on the mind in the same manner with those, which the senses, memory or reason present to us. But as education is an artificial and not a natural cause, and its maxims are frequently contrary to reason, and even to themselves in different times and places, it is never upon that account recogniz'd by philosophers; tho' in reality it be built almost on the same foundation of custom and repetition as our reasonings from causes and effects.

(1978:117)

Here the narrow sense of imagination is again contrasted with judgement, and also with reason, which latter is taken to include causal inference. And education, as one of the processes of narrow imagination is described as 'never recognised by philosophers'.

Hume provides a clarification in a footnote in which again causal inference is contrasted favourably with the processes of narrow imagination:

In general we may observe, that as our assent to all probable reasonings is founded on the vivacity of ideas, it resembles many of those whimsies and prejudices, which are rejected under the opprobrious character of being the offspring of the imagination. By this expression it appears that the word imagination, is commonly used in two different senses; and tho' nothing be more contrary to true philosophy, than this inaccuracy, yet in the following reasonings I have often been oblig'd to fall into it. When I oppose the imagination to the memory, I mean the faculty by which we form our fainter ideas. When I oppose it to reason I mean the same faculty, excluding only our demonstrative and probable reasonings.

(1978:117)

Thus, we see that Hume, when he is being careful with his terminology, distinguishes two senses of imagination: a broad sense which includes what he calls judgement or reason, including causal inference, and a narrow sense whose activities he compares unfavourably with those of judgement or reason. It is hard to read this otherwise than, as Loeb puts it, assigning 'causal inference normative pride of place' (1995a:104). The evidence so far thus suggests that the widespread acceptance of the traditional reading of Hume as a sceptic about induction is merely a product of our 'education' (in Hume's sense of the word).

As Broughton and Loeb both point out, further support for this contention can be found in the distinction Hume draws between 'proofs' and 'probabilities' in Section 11 of Part III, the distinction between 'philosophical' and 'unphilosophical' probabilities in Section 13, and the 'Rules by which to Judge of Causes and Effects' offered in Section 15.

Earlier in Part III Hume uses 'probability' to cover all arguments from causation. But in Section 11 he draws a distinction between 'proofs' which are 'arguments from causation' which 'exceed probability and may be received as a superior kind of evidence' and 'probability' – 'that evidence which is still attended with uncertainty' (1978:124). Thus, *within* the class of causal inferences, Hume here draws a distinction between better and worse arguments, an odd thing to do if, as Stroud puts it, he thinks that: 'As far as the competition for degrees of reasonableness is concerned, all beliefs about the unobserved are tied for last place' (1977:54).

More tellingly, perhaps, Hume introduces a distinction in Section 13 between 'philosophical' and 'unphilosophical' probabilities. The former are 'received by philosophers and allowed to be reasonable foundations of belief and opinion' (1978:143). The latter, though 'derived from the same principles ... have not had the good fortune to obtain the same sanction' (1978:143). Hume's first illustration of unphilosophical probability is the manner in which an argument is more persuasive if founded on a recently remembered fact:

> The argument, which we found on any matter of fact we remember, is more or less convincing, according as the fact is recent or remote; and tho' the difference in these degrees of existence be not receiv'd by philosophy as solid and legitimate; because in that case an argument must have a different force today, from

what it shall have a month hence; yet notwithstanding the opposition of philosophy, 'tis certain, this circumstance has a
considerable influence on the understanding.

(1978:143)

Of course, Hume does not say here that the differences in degrees of
evidence are *not* solid and legitimate, he merely says that they are not
received by *philosophers* as such. This passage can then be read in a
way that is consistent with the traditional reading of Hume as a
sceptic about induction if we read him here as distancing himself from
'the philosophers' – merely describing their views but not endorsing
them.

It is hard to sustain this reading of Section 13, however. First,
Hume *does* sometimes speak in his own voice in commenting
unfavourably on unphilosophical probability, as here:

A fourth unphilosophical species of probability is that derived
from *general rules*, which we rashly form to ourselves, and which
are the source of what we properly call PREJUDICE. An *Irishman*
cannot have wit, and a *Frenchman* cannot have solidity; for which
reason, tho' the conversation of the former in any instance be
visibly very agreeable, and of the latter very judicious, we have
entertained such a prejudice against them, that they must be
dunces or fops in spite of sense and reason. Human nature is very
subject to error of this kind; and perhaps, this nation as much as
any other.

(1978:146–7)

Second, throughout this section Hume observes the distinction
drawn earlier between the judgement and narrow imagination, and
ascribes unphilosophical probabilities to the imagination:

the present subject of [philosophical] probabilities offers us [an]
obvious [instance], ... in the opposition betwixt the judgement and
imagination ... According to my system all reasonings are nothing
but the effects of custom, and custom has no influence, but by
inlivening the imagination ... It may, therefore be concluded that

our judgement and imagination can never be contrary ... This difficulty we can remove after no other manner, than by supposing the influence of general rules ... By them we learn to distinguish the accidental circumstances from the efficacious causes; and when we find that an effect can be produced without ... any particular circumstance, we conclude that that circumstance makes no part of the efficacious cause, however frequently conjoin'd with it. But as this frequent conjunction necessarily makes it have some effect on the imagination, in spite of the opposite conclusion from general rules ... [we] ascribe the one inference to our judgement, and the other to our imagination. The general rule is attributed to our judgement; as being more extensive and constant. The exception to the imagination; as being more capricious and uncertain.

(1978:149)

In the light of Hume's earlier unfavourable comments on the imagination in contrast to the judgement or reason, which, occurring only twenty-two pages earlier, he cannot have forgotten or expected his reader to forget, the careful distinction maintained here between the two is further evidence that Hume is prepared to side with 'the philosophers' in their negative assessment of unphilosophical probability.

The final piece of evidence from Part III in support of the rejection of the traditional view of Hume as a sceptic about induction is Section 15 ('Rules by which to Judge of Causes and Effects'). These rules are the 'general rules' referred to in the passage just quoted, which enable us to make the distinction between judgement and narrow imagination, and they are described by Hume as enabling us to '*know* when [objects] *really* are [causes or effects to each other]' (1978:173, my emphasis). Again, this passage can be read by supporters of the traditional interpretation, with more or less strain, in a way that accords with their view of Hume. But the cumulative case provided by the passages cited is, I submit, very impressive, and is further strengthened by subsequent material in Part IV.

Here the crucial sections for our purposes are Section 3, Section 4 and Section 7. In Section 3 ('Of the Ancient Philosophy') Hume turns to an examination of the psychological mechanism by which the ancient philosophers arrived at their beliefs in substances, forms, accidents and occult qualities. His tone throughout is one of superiority; his aim simply to discover the causes in human nature which led the ancient philosophers to their 'unreasonable and capricious' fictions (1978:219) and made them produce a system of philosophy which is 'entirely incomprehensible' (1978:224). In Section 4 ('Of the Modern Philosophy') he begins by responding to an objection which he thinks these criticisms of the ancient philosophers might prompt:

> It may be objected that the imagination, according to my own confession, being the ultimate judge of all systems of philosophy, I am unjust in blaming the ancient philosophers for making use of that faculty, and allowing themselves to be entirely guided by it in their reasonings.
>
> (1978:225)

His response is to make explicit the distinction we have seen him operating with consistently between the two sets of mechanisms in wide imagination:

> the principles which are permanent, irresistable, and universal; such as the customary transition from causes to effects, and from effects to causes; And the principles, which are changeable, weak and irregular; such as those I have just now taken notice of. The former are the foundation of all our thoughts and actions, so that upon their removal human nature must immediately perish and go to ruin. The latter are neither unavoidable to mankind, nor necessary, or so much as useful in the conduct of life; but on the contrary are observ'd only to take place in weak minds, and being opposite to the other principles of custom and reasoning, may easily be subverted by a due contrast and opposition. For this reason the former are received by philosophy and the latter rejected.
>
> (1978:225)

Here, at last, Hume provides a basis for his preference for causal inference over the mechanisms of belief formation which he refuses to allow as belonging to reason in contradistinction to the imagination. The former is an indispensable component of our psychology and its action irresistible; the latter are neither indispensable nor incapable of being resisted. It is for this reason that the ancient philosophers can rightly be criticized for their incomprehensible systems. 'A little reflection' (1978:224) was all that was needed to suppress the inclinations that led them to their fantasies, and their failure so to reflect was a signal weakness for which there can be no excuse. Thus, Hume is able to say, it is indeed true that both causal inference and the mechanisms of the narrow imagination which led the ancient philosophers to their fictions are at once components of our human nature and mechanisms of the imagination in the wide sense; nevertheless they can be clearly distinguished:

> One who concludes somebody to be near him, when he hears an articulate voice in the dark, reasons justly and naturally; tho' that conclusion be derived from nothing but custom ... on account of [the] usual conjunction with the present impression. But one, who is tormented he knows not why, with the apprehension of spectres in the dark, may, perhaps, be said to reason, and to reason naturally, too: But then it must be in the same sense, that a malady is said to be natural; as arising from natural causes, tho' it be contrary to health, the most agreeable and natural situation of man ... The opinions of the ancient philosophers ... are like the spectres in the dark, and are derived from principles which are ... neither universal nor unavoidable in human nature.
>
> (1978:225–6)

So far, then, the reading of Hume as a sceptic, who denies any distinction between good and bad reasoning, and, in particular, denies that causal inference is any better than any other mechanism of belief formation, seems unwarranted.

However, Hume *is* a sceptic and the basis for his scepticism emerges in the immediately following paragraph of Section 4. It is, however, a basis for scepticism which is quite different from the basis of scepticism appealed to by the traditional interpretation. For, in fact, the mechanisms of narrow imagination which produce the ancient philosophers' belief in the fictions of substance and accident are *identical* with the psychological mechanisms which produce our belief in an external world. But belief in an external world, as Hume has explained in the previous Section 2 ('Of Scepticism with regard to the Senses'), far from being something which can be suppressed by a little reflection, is inescapable: 'Nature has not left that to ... choice ... 'Tis vain to ask, *whether there be body or not*? That is a point which we must take for granted in all our reasoning.' (1978:187). The mechanisms of the imagination in question *are* therefore permanent, irresistible and unavoidable, after all, and the foundation of Hume's division between the principles received by philosophers and those which are not is thus undermined. Moreover, it turns out, as Hume's argument proceeds, that causal inference not only does not provide support for our belief in an external world, as Hume has emphasized in Section 2, but, further, directly opposes that belief: 'there is a direct and total opposition betwixt our reason and our sense; or more properly speaking, betwixt those conclusions we form from cause and effect, and those that persuade us of the continu'd and independent existence of body' (1978:231). Thus, Hume concludes, two sets of psychological mechanisms are in direct opposition: those, on the one hand, that he had previously ascribed to the understanding or reason, which include causal inference as a central component, and those, on the other hand, that he had previously ascribed to narrow imagination and had regarded as operative only on weak minds. Both these sets of psychological mechanisms are irresistible in their influence and so no distinction can be drawn between them. So, indeed, no belief can be regarded as more justified than any other.

This is the basis of Hume's scepticism in Part IV. And in the final section of Part IV, in which he tries to find a way forward past the 'manifold contradictions and imperfections in human reason' (1978: 268) he has uncovered, it is the conflict exposed in Section 4 (to which a footnote refers us), rather than the argument of Section 6 of Part III (as the traditional sceptical interpretation would lead us to expect) which is the starting point of his descent into pessimism. The argument of Section 6 of Part III, in which (according to the traditional interpretation) Hume establishes to his own satisfaction the irrationality of causal inference, receives nothing like so prominent a mention. And in the allusions made to it ('After the most accurate and exact of my reasonings, I can give no reason why I should assent to it … Experience … instructs me in the several conjunctions of objects for the past. Habit … determines me to expect the same for the future … Without this quality … which seemingly is so trivial and so little founded on reason … we could never assent to any argument' (1978:265)), his language is entirely consistent with the thorough-going causal literalist interpretation defended above ('is founded on reason', for example, can be read as 'is the effect of reason'; compare the use of 'founded on' in the first paragraph (1978:90)).

I conclude that the non-traditional interpretation of Section 6 of Part III offered here, according to which Hume is not to be understood as arguing for a version of scepticism about induction, at least fits as comfortably with the text of the final section of Part IV as the traditional one. And, as we have seen, it can be further supported from earlier sections of Part IV and from Part III itself. We now need to consider the positive phase of Hume's account of the manner in which we extend our beliefs to unobserved matters of fact.

The nature and causes of belief

So far Hume's argument has been entirely negative. His conclusion, as we have seen, is that:

> not only our reason fails us in the discovery of the *ultimate connexion* of causes and effects, but even after experience has inform'd us of their *constant conjunction*, 'tis impossible for us to satisfy ourselves by our reason, why we should extend that experience beyond these particular instances which have fallen under our observation.
>
> (1978:92)

Hume infers that our inferential practices are not the product of reason but have another explanation:

> When the mind, therefore, passes from the idea or impression of one object to the idea or belief of another, it is not determined by

> reason, but by certain principles, which associate together the ideas
> of these objects and unite them in the imagination.
>
> (1978:92)

It is a fact, Hume thinks, that we do make inferences from the observed to the unobserved. And it is also a fact that we make such inferences only after we have observed a constant conjunction of two sorts of thing and are presented with a thing of one of these sorts. We make such a transition in such circumstances simply because there is operative in the human mind a 'principle of union' of ideas to the effect that: 'when ev'ry individual of any species is found by experience to be constantly united with an individual of another species, the appearance of any new individual of either species naturally conveys the thought to its usual attendant' (1978:93).

Thus it is just a fact about human beings that they are so constituted that experience of a constant conjunction of A's and B's will create in them a disposition to form an idea of an A when presented with an idea of a B and conversely. The creation of this disposition is not a rational product of the mind and, in particular, Hume is anxious to stress, its creation will not be a result of the mind's noting or reflecting on the fact that all A's have been conjoined with B's. The brute fact of the constant conjunction of A's and B's in experience (that is, the bare fact of the occurrence of that pattern in experience), independently of its being known or reflected on, will suffice to create the disposition:

> the past experience on which all our judgements concerning cause
> and effect depend, may operate on the mind in such an insensible
> manner as never to be taken notice of and may even, in some sense,
> be unknown to us. A person who stops short in his journey upon
> meeting a river in his way, foresees the consequences of his
> proceeding forward; and his knowledge of these consequences is
> conveyed to him by past experience, which informs him of such
> certain conjunctions of causes and effects. But can we think that
> on this occasion he reflects on any past experience, and calls to
> remembrance instances that he has seen or heard of, in order to
> discover the effects of water on animal bodies? No surely ... the

idea of sinking is so closely connected with that of water, and the idea of suffocating with that of sinking, that the mind makes the transition without the assistance of the memory. The custom operates before we have time for reflexion ... we must necessarily acknowledge that experience may produce a belief and a judgement of causes and effects by a secret operation, and without once being thought of. This removes all pretext ... for asserting that the mind is convinc'd by reasoning of that principle, *that instances of which we have no experience, must necessarily resemble those of which we have.* For we here find that the understanding or imagination can draw inferences from past experience without reflecting on it; much more without forming any principle concerning it, or reasoning upon that principle.

(1978:103–4)

Hume reinforces this point in the final section of Part III ('Of the Reason of Animals'). He observes at the beginning of the section that no truth appears to him to be more evident than that beasts are endowed with thought and reason as well as men. For, like men, beasts adopt means to ends in seeking self-preservation, obtaining pleasure and avoiding pain. Hence, Hume says, we must ascribe these actions to the same causes (that is, thought and reasoning) as in the case of human beings. Consequently, Hume goes on, there is

a kind of touchstone by which we may try every system in this species of philosophy ... when any hypothesis ... is advanc'd to explain a mental operation, which is common to men and beasts, we must apply the same hypothesis to both; and as every true hypothesis will abide by this trial, so ... no false one will ever be able to endure it.

(1978:176–7)

But consider now a dog 'that avoids fires and precipices, that shuns strangers and caresses his master' (1978:177). Such actions, Hume claims, proceed from a process of reasoning that is not itself different from that which appears in human nature. But:

beasts certainly never perceive any real connexion among objects. 'Tis therefore by experience they infer one from another. They can never by any arguments form a general conclusion, that those objects, of which they have had no experience, resemble those of which they have. 'Tis therefore by means of custom alone that experience operates upon them. All this was sufficiently evident with respect to man. But with respect to beasts there cannot be the least suspicion of mistake; which must be owned to be a strong confirmation or rather an invincible proof, of my system.

(1978:178)

The interesting question to ask here is why Hume thinks the facts he here cites about brutes constitute an 'invincible proof' of his system. What they do show is that the disposition to infer causes from effects and vice versa after an observed constant conjunction is not in beasts the product of an argument in which the Uniformity Principle figures as a premiss. Given Hume's 'touchstone' he is entitled to conclude that the same is true of human beings. But this, on the literalist interpretation given above, is just the conclusion of Hume's argument in Section 6. The alternative, traditional, interpretation of that section as putting forward a sceptical argument against the rationality of induction, has to interpret Hume's claim about the 'invincible proof' provided to his system by the facts he cites as indicative of a total failure to appreciate the ambitious nature of his argument in Section 6, whose conclusion could not possibly (on the traditional interpretation) be established by any purely causal considerations of the type Hume cites (it is for the same reason, of course, that the summary passage quoted above from the first *Enquiry* (1975:39) is a challenge to the traditional interpretation). Once again, then, Hume's text provides support for the interpretation defended above.

So far, however, Hume has only explained how an *idea* of a B will occur to a man who has been exposed to a constant conjunction of A's and B's when an idea of an A is present to his mind. But when, after being exposed to such a constant conjunction, a man gets an *impression* of an A, he will not just form the *idea* of a B; a *belief* that a B will actually occur will come to be present in his mind. Hence, Hume needs to explain how that happens, and to do that he has to explain how a belief differs from a mere idea. This is the task of Section 7.

That there is such a difference is evident. I can think of something, say a unicorn, have an idea of it, without believing in its existence. Or again, you may tell me something which I do not believe – say, that Caesar died in his bed – such that I can then understand perfectly what you say, in Hume's words (1978:95) 'form and conjoin' all the ideas you 'form and conjoin', without actually believing you. In fact, there are three notions to be considered, but because of the domination of his thought by the theory of ideas Hume conflates two of them. First, there is the mere *thinking about* something, or conception. Second, there is the entertaining in thought of a propositional content – *that* something is the case. And finally there is belief. Hume conflates the first two because, in general, he cannot distinguish complex ideas and propositions, and (in the particular case of existential propositions) he cannot even distinguish *simple* ideas from propositions since he denies any distinct idea of existence and therefore insists that we can form a proposition containing only one idea (1978:97). Thus his enquiry is directed at the distinction between, on the one hand, thinking about something or entertaining a propositional content (not distinguished) and, on the other hand, believing that something is the case. It is this question he formulates as: 'Wherein consists the difference betwixt incredulity and belief?' (1978:95).

Hume's discussion proceeds in two stages. First, he explains what the difference cannot be, and then he goes on, in the light of this, to explain what the difference *must* be. What the difference cannot be, he argues, is that believing something as opposed to merely entertaining an idea or proposition involves the presence of an extra idea – perhaps the idea of existence or reality. The thought that P and the belief that P do not differ in their content. When I move from doubting whether P to believing that P, what I later believe is the very same thing that I previously doubted. (This is something Hume is bound to accept because of his identification of ideas, *qua* thought constituents, with images. But independently of his theory, the point is still undeniable.) Moreover, even setting aside the first point, there is no idea whose addition to others *could* make the difference between merely enter-taining a thought and believing it. Even if there is a genuine distinct idea of existence (which Hume denies), for example, it could not accomplish this. For one can *entertain* the thought that God exists as easily as believing that God exists. Furthermore, Hume argues, the mind has control over all its ideas 'and therefore if believing consisted in some idea, which we add to the simple conception, it would be in a man's power by adding this idea to it, to believe any thing, which he can conceive' (1978:653). Thus, Hume concludes, the difference between merely entertaining a thought and believing it cannot be a difference in content – a difference in what is before the mind of the thinker – it can only be a difference in the *manner* of conception. But, Hume now goes on, the only variation an idea can survive without being changed into another idea is a variation in degree of force or vivacity – hence, as belief does nothing but vary the manner in which we conceive any object, it can only bestow on our ideas an additional force or vivacity. 'An opinion, therefore, or belief, may be most accurately defin'd, A LIVELY IDEA RELATED TO OR ASSOCIATED WITH A PRESENT IMPRESSION' (1978:96).

It is hard not to feel dissatisfied with this account of belief, and Hume himself indicates his dissatisfaction with it in the 'Appendix' to the *Treatise* (though, it should be noted, the two oddities which modern commentators most often point out – that the account is an account only of belief in an occurrent sense, whereas 'belief' is most commonly a term for a dispositional state, and that Hume implies that liveliness brought about otherwise than by a relatedness to a present impression does *not* constitute belief – are clearly *not* the source of Hume's dissatisfaction there; what is, however, is totally unclear). In the body of the *Treatise*, however, Hume claims that the definition 'is entirely conformable to everyone's feeling and experience' (1978:97). But his attempt to illustrate it only brings out the inadequacy of the language in which he attempts to express the distinction:

If one person sits down to read a book as a romance and another as a true history, they plainly receive the same ideas, and in the same order, nor does the incredulity of the one, and the belief of the other, hinder them from putting the very same sense upon their author. His words produce the same ideas in both; tho' his testimony has not the same influence on them. The latter has a more lively conception of all the incidents. He enters deeper into the concerns of the persons; represents to himself their actions and characters and friendships and enmities: he even goes so far as to form a notion of their features, and air and person. While the former, who gives no credit to the testimony of the author, has a more faint and languid conception of all these particulars, and except on account of the style and ingenuity of the composition can receive little entertainment from it.

(1978:17–18)

The first half of this passage rests on the point on which Hume is absolutely clear: that the very same perception may be entertained in thought, with and without belief. The second half of the passage attempts to explain what this distinction consists in and is an evident failure. Of course, a person reading a fiction need not have such a 'faint and languid conception' of the incidents as Hume here supposes; of course, he may form a notion of the 'features and air and person' of the characters and 'represent to himself their actions and characters, friendships and enmities'. If we understand the notions of vividness and liveliness in any familiar sense, then, Hume's account is woefully inadequate.

But even if we set this point aside, Hume's account of belief still faces obvious problems. One is that Hume is using the same notion of vivacity to distinguish beliefs from ideas as he previously used to distinguish impressions from ideas. Beliefs, however, are not impressions, so their degree of vivacity must fall somewhat in between that of impressions and that of ideas. But where, exactly? What degree of vivacity marks the boundary between an impression and a belief, and what degree marks the boundary between a belief and an idea? Hume simply does not say, and, of course, there is nothing in his system to provide any basis for decision, since the notion of vivacity remains wholly metaphorical.

In fact, the situation is even worse, for Hume has to fit memories into his system, and again the only notion he has to appeal to is that of vivacity. Thus memories come into the picture as less vivid than impressions but more vivid than beliefs, which are, in turn, more vivid than mere ideas. But the idea that all of these differ simply in respect of variations along a single dimension is absurd. Memories are essentially past directed, and an increase in the vivacity attaching to a future-directed proposition could never transform it from a belief about the future to a memory of the past. This difference is, in fact, a difference in *content*, rather than in *manner* of conception, as Hume would have it, and Hume's thinking otherwise is again simply a consequence of his viewing the phenomenon through the distorting spectacles of the theory of ideas, within which no adequate account of tense is possible.

Nevertheless, despite these difficulties with his definition of belief as a vivid idea, it is an important part, for Hume, of his explanation of what is involved in causal inference. For it enables him to explain the transition from the observation of a cause to the belief in the effect as a case of a more general phenomenon: vivacity communication via the association of ideas. He says:

> I wou'd willingly establish it as a general maxim in the science of human nature *that when any impression becomes present to us, it not only transports the mind to such ideas as are related to it, but likewise communicates to them a share of its force and vivacity.*

> (1978:98)

Notice that this principle can only explain the origin of belief if beliefs are distinguished from mere ideas by the possession, in a higher degree than mere ideas, of a quality that is *also* possessed, in a still higher degree, by impressions. Thus, despite the absurdity noted above of trying to describe the differences among ideas, beliefs, memories and impressions, by locating them within different regions of a one-dimensional scale measuring 'degrees of vivacity', this is precisely what Hume needs to do. For otherwise he would have no *explanation* at all of what is going on in causal inference, but a mere *description* of the process.

Section 8 of Part III is devoted to arguing for and illustrating the general principle of vivacity transference. Hume argues that not only the cause–effect link (revealed, by now, to be dependent on observed constant conjunction), but also the two other principles of association, resemblance and contiguity, can produce an enlivening of ideas.

But, as we have seen, he insists that these other two principles cannot produce a sufficient degree of liveliness in an associated idea to transform it into a belief. For otherwise it would not be the case that: ''Tis only causation, which produces such a connexion, as to give us assurance, from the existence or action of one object, that 'twas followed or preceded by any other existence or action' (1978:73–4).

The explanation of this difference, Hume suggests, is, in essence, that causes are necessary and sufficient conditions of their effects. Thus, whereas 'there is no manner of necessity for the mind to feign any resembling, and contiguous object; and if it feigns such, there is so little necessity for it always to confine itself to the same, without any difference or variation' (1978:109), the 'relation of cause and effect':

> has all the opposite advantages. The objects it presents are fixt and unalterable. The impressions of the memory never change in any considerable degree; and each impression draws along with it a precise idea, which takes its place in the imagination, as something solid and real, certain and invariable. The thought is always determin'd to pass from the impression to the idea, and from that particular impression to that particular idea, without any choice or hesitation.
>
> (1978:110)

But, Hume insists, though in this way causal inference is a special case, transitions made via resemblance and contiguity can still *add to* the liveliness of the idea arrived at, and where such an additional effect is *not* present belief is correspondingly less firm and hesitant.

He finds here an explanation of the hold on philosophers of the belief that causes and effects must be resembling and necessarily connected. Where causes and effects *are* resembling, as in the communication of motion by impulse, our belief in the effect, given the cause, is greatly strengthened and in consequence 'some philosophers have imagin'd … that a reasonable man might immediately infer the motion of one object from the impulse of another, without having recourse to any past observation' (1978:111). But really this is not so; it is just another illustration of the vivacity-transferring power of resemblance. On the other hand, where cause and effect are *not* resembling, the opposite effect occurs, 'as resemblance, where conjoin'd with causation, fortifies our reasonings; so the want of it in any very great degree is able almost entirely to destroy them' (1978:113), and some may find it impossible to believe that there is a causal link at all.

This, then, in sum, is Hume's account of how our beliefs in matters of fact are to be explained. They are not, at bottom, a product of reasoning, but of the imagination, and explicable by general principles of natural functioning. They are derived from nothing but custom, and belief 'is more properly an act of the sensitive than of the cogitative part of our natures' (1978:183).

The idea of necessary connection

The long discussion of the inference from the observed to the unobserved is supposed to be a detour on the road to discovering the idea of necessary connection. We can find no impression of necessary connection in any particular pairing of cause and effect, so the origin of the idea remains obscure. In explaining why he planned to concentrate on the inference from the observed to the unobserved Hume hinted that: 'Perhaps 'twill appear in the end, that the necessary connexion depends on the inference, instead of the inference depending on the necessary connexion' (1978:88).

Of course, this is just how it does turn out.

So far, as we have seen, Hume has appealed to constant conjunction to explain how beliefs about the unobserved arise through causal inference. But the origin of the idea of necessary connection has not yet been accounted for. However, Hume thinks, constant conjunction can be brought in here also. In each instance of a causal connection we simply observe one thing following another and we get no impression of necessary connection. Only after repeated observations of instances of the cause–effect link do we get the idea of necessary connection. But:

'tis evident, in the first place, that the repetition of like objects in like relations of succession and contiguity *discovers* nothing new in any one of them … Second, 'tis certain that this repetition of similar objects ... *produces* nothing new either in these objects, or in any external body. For ... the several instances we have of the conjunction of resembling causes and effects are in themselves entirely independent ... They are entirely divided by time and place: and the one might have existed ... tho' the other never had been in being.

(1978:81)

How then can the observation of repeated instances of a cause–effect link explain the origin of the idea of necessary connection? Hume's answer is that though the several resembling instances can 'never produce any new quality in the *object*, which can be the model of that idea, yet the *observation* of this resemblance, produces a new impression *in the mind*, which is its real model' (1978:165). This new impression is an *impression of reflection* whose occurrence in the mind is an accompaniment of the movement which takes place, after an observed constant conjunction, from the idea or impression of the cause to the idea of (or belief in) the effect.

In Hume's own words:

After we have observed the resemblance in a sufficient number of instances we immediately feel a determination of the mind to pass from one object to its usual attendant, and to consider it in a stronger light upon account of that relation. This determination is the only effect of the resemblance, and, therefore, must be the same with power or efficacy, whose idea is derived from that resemblance. The several instances of resembling conjunctions leads us into the notion of power or necessity. These instances are in themselves totally distinct from each other, and have no union but in the mind which observes them and collects their ideas. Necessity, then, is the effect of this observation, and is nothing but an internal impression of the mind, or a determination to carry our thoughts from one object to another.

(1978:165)

Part of what Hume wishes to say here is clear, but there are difficulties with it. He says that the only new thing that occurs in the mind after the repeated observation of B's following A's is a *determination* of the mind to pass from one object to its usual attendant and to conceive it in a new light on account of that relation. What he means is that having repeatedly observed B's following A's we are *caused* by the next observation of an A to expect a B. That is, the complex mental event *an observed constant conjunction of A's with B's + an impression of an A* causes *a belief in a B* to occur. But that is not all. In addition a *feeling of determination* is produced which accompanies the transition to the belief in a B, and this is the impression of reflection.

But what is this feeling of determination? First, although Hume sometimes writes as if this is so, it is *not* 'the determination' of the mind itself. The latter is simply the transition of the mind from one idea to another which is produced by the observation of constant conjunction (or, rather, by the constant observation of conjunction), that is, the *fact* that an idea of an A is followed by an idea of a B, or the *event* that consists in the occurrence of an idea of an A in the mind followed by an idea of a B. The determination of the mind is, therefore, of the wrong logical category to be itself an impression, that is, a perception. The fact that one perception is followed by another, or the event consisting in one perception's being followed by another cannot itself be a perception. Second, the feeling of determination is not an impression *of* a necessary connection obtaining between the complex cause event – *observing a constant conjunction of A's and B's + perceiving an A* – and the effect event – *believing in the imminent occurrence (forming a lively idea) of a B*. For Hume's thesis is that a necessary connection is never observable between distinct events whether they be mental or physical, since no two distinct events are necessarily connected.

In fact, Hume is insistent that we can no more get the idea of necessary connection by observing causal linkages in the mental realm than we can get it by observing causal linkages in the physical realm. The 'feeling of determination' Hume refers to can, therefore, only be an *accompaniment* to the transition from the idea of an A to the idea of a B. We may try to understand it as a feeling of helplessness or inevitability that occurs in the mind when the disposition to make the transition from an idea of an A to the idea of a B, which has been produced by a constant observation of A's with B's, is activated by the occurrence in the mind of an idea of an A. It is, therefore, only a *contingent fact* that it occurs when such a transition takes place since anything can cause anything and anything can fail to cause anything – a feature of it which Hume disguises from himself by his language, which consistently makes the impossible identification of the impression of necessary connection with the 'determination of the mind' or 'the transition arising from the accustomed union' or the 'propensity, which custom produces, to pass from an object to the idea of its usual attendant' (1978:165). The idea of necessity, then, has its origin in an impression of reflection, and so: 'Upon the whole, necessity is something, that exists in the mind, not in objects; nor is it possible for us ever to form the most distant idea of it, considered as a quality in bodies' (1978:165–6).

But we ascribe necessity to objects nonetheless. Hence Hume still has to explain this mistake. Once again he does so by appealing to a general property of the human mind which can be appealed to in other cases, too – the propensity of the mind 'to spread itself on external objects, and to conjoin with them any internal impressions, which they occasion, and which always make their appearances at the same time that these objects discover themselves to the senses' (1978:167).

This propensity is appealed to by Hume in two other places, one of which (Part IV, Section 5) is footnoted at this point. The other, to which a Section 5 footnote refers us back, is Section 2 of Part IV. In Section 5 of Part IV Hume appeals to this propensity to explain our belief that sounds and smells, which have no spatial location, are located in the same place as certain visible and extended objects. If we consider a fig at one end of a table and an olive at the other, he says, we evidently conjoin the bitter taste of the one and the sweet taste of the other with the coloured and tangible qualities of these objects. Thus we suppose the bitter taste to be located at one end of the table and the sweet at the other, though in reality they have no spatial location whatsoever. The explanation of this is the following:

Tho' an extended object be incapable of a conjunction in place with another, that exists without any place or extension, yet they are susceptible of many other relations. Thus the taste and smell of any fruit are inseparable from its other qualities of colour and tangibility; and whichever of them be the cause or effect, 'tis certain they are always co-existent. Nor are they only co-existent in general, but also co-temporary in their appearance in the mind; and 'tis upon the application of the extended body to our senses we perceive its particular taste and smell. These relations, then, of *causation*, and *contiguity in the time of their appearance*, betwixt the extended object and the quality, which exists without any particular place, must have such an effect on the mind, that upon the appearance of one it will immediately turn its thought to the conception of the other. Nor is this all. We not only turn our thought from one to the other upon account of their relation, but likewise endeavour to give them a new relation, *viz.* that of *a conjunction in place*, that we may render the transition more easy and natural. For 'tis a quality ... in human nature ... that when objects are united by any relation, we have a strong propensity to add some new relation to them, in order to compleat the union.

(1978:237)

Hume appeals to this same phenomenon to explain why we, or rather, the (Lockean) philosophers who distinguish external objects from their perceptions, believe that the particular external objects resemble the perceptions they cause – because they add the relation of resemblance to that of causation 'to compleat the union', and we can now see how it enables him likewise to explain our 'spreading the mind on the world' in the case of necessary connection. For here, just as in the case of tastes, the internal impression of reflection, which gives rise to the idea of necessity, is *caused* by the external situation, and *contiguous in the time of its appearance*. We therefore add the relation of *conjunction in place* to complete the union and render the transition more natural, that is, we ascribe an external spatial location *between* the objects to the necessary connection we have an idea of, though in doing so, as in the case of tastes, we are ascribing a location to something which really exists nowhere.

Later in the *Treatise*, and elsewhere in Hume's writings, the propensity to 'spread our mind on the world' is also invoked by Hume to explain our ascriptions of moral and aesthetic qualities to things.

Just as in the case of necessity these qualities cannot be found *in* the objects or situations to which we ascribe them:

> Take any action allow'd to be vicious: wilful murder, for instance. Examine it in all lights, and see if you can find that matter of fact, or real existence, which you call *vice*. In whichever way you take it, you find only certain passions, motives, volitions and thoughts. There is no other matter of fact in the case. The vice entirely escapes you, as long as you consider the object.
>
> (1978:248)

Again, in the case of beauty, as Hume explains in his essay 'The Sceptic':

> EUCLID has fully explained every quality of the circle, but has not, in any proposition, said a word of its beauty. The reason is evident. Beauty is not a quality of the circle. It lies not in any part of the line whose parts are all equally distant from a common centre ... In vain would you look for it in the circle, or seek it, either by your senses or by mathematical reasonings, in all the properties of that figure.
>
> (1948:343)

And, in general:

> If we can depend upon any principle which we learn from philosophy, this, I think, may be considered as certain and undoubted: that there is nothing, in itself, valuable or despicable, desirable or hateful, beautiful or deformed.
>
> (1948:340)

The explanation of our ascribing such qualities to objects is that in each case, on contemplating the relevant object we feel a certain sentiment – an impression of reflection. Thus, in the case of wilful murder, you can never find the vice:

till you turn your reflexion into your own breast, and find a sentiment of disapprobation, which arises in you, towards this action.

(1978:469)

As for beauty:

It is only the effect which that figure produces upon a mind whose
particular fabric or structure renders it capable of such sentiments.

(1948:343)

And in general, all aesthetic and moral attributes:

arise from the particular constitution or fabric of human sentiment and affection.

(1948:340)

In each case what happens is precisely parallel to what happens,
according to Hume, in the case of necessary connection. A certain
impression of reflection is produced in the mind and the mind (or,
more precisely, the imagination) then conjoins the internal impression
with the external object that occasions it, displaying, to use a new
metaphor introduced in the *Enquiry Concerning the Principles of
Morals*:

a productive faculty, and gilding or staining all natural objects with
the colours, borrowed from internal sentiment, rais[ing] in a
manner a new creation.

(1975:294)

This propensity, to project the internal impressions of the mind on-
to external objects, is thus a very important one for Hume, but it is not
easy to understand the process or to give uncontroversial examples of
its application. What might seem a clear example is given by A.H.
Basson:

A clear case of projection occurred during the last war, when
people wrote to the newspapers complaining of the gloomy and

despondent note put forth by air raid sirens. Why, they asked, could not the authorities have arranged for these to play some cheerful and encouraging tune, like 'Britannia Rules the Waves'? The answer was, of course, that the note of the sirens was not despondent or alarming, but its acquired associations induced despondency in the listener. Even if they had played 'Britannia Rules the Waves' people would soon have complained of a hitherto unsuspected menace in that tune. The projection was, in fact, nearly complete for most people: the warning note was actually felt as menacing, and the note at the end of the raid really sounded cheerful. But it could have been the other way round, and so we are intellectually convinced that the warning note was not in itself menacing, although it became impossible to imagine or to feel it as otherwise.

(1958: 66–7)

It is, of course, clear what mistake was being made by the writers to the newspapers in this entertaining story. They thought that the note made by the siren produced feelings of despondency in them, and would have done so even if it had *not* been associated, as it was, with the prospect of imminent death and disaster. So they thought that the note had a certain dispositional property: being such as to produce certain effects in human hearers. And their mistake was in thinking that this dispositional property was possessed by the note independently of its association with wartime circumstances. But, of course, the note *could* have had such an unconditional dispositional property, for, as we know from Hume, anything can cause anything. Thus, it might have been that the writers to the newspapers were right and the authorities had chosen as a warning note a sound which, as it happened, possibly because of facts of human evolution, *would* produce feelings of depression in *any* normal human being, even in the most euphoric circumstances.

If our mistake, then, in 'spreading our minds on the world' and ascribing a necessary connection to causes and effects themselves, is analogous to the mistake made by Basson's writers to the newspapers, our belief in such a necessary connection in the objects, though false, will only be *contingently* false, and the same will be true, *mutatis mutandis*, of our ascriptions of moral and aesthetic qualities to objects, which Hume thinks of as products of the same mechanism. Now, of course, we *can* make such mistakes about the dispositions of external objects to affect human beings: finding something disgusting or boring, I might naively think that everyone will so do, that is, that the object has a disposition to produce that effect in every human being. And, if I discover that its power is less general than I supposed, all I will learn, like Basson's newspaper writers, if they were ever persuaded of their mistake, is that *as a matter of fact* my original belief, though possibly true, was, in fact, mistaken.

Similarly, given that there is an impression of necessary connection which is produced in one's mind in the circumstances Hume supposes (that is, when one has encountered a constant conjunction of A's with B's and is currently aware of an A) it would be possible to think that that impression of reflection had a less complex cause – for example, the mere observation of an A. And this mistake *would* be parallel to the mistake made by the newspaper writers who complained about the sound chosen as the siren warning note.

But this is not the mistake Hume has in mind when he speaks of 'spreading our minds on the world'. For this mistaken belief, like that of the newspaper writers, *could* have been true. For Hume, however, the ascription of necessity to objects is as absurd as the ascription of spatial location to sounds and tastes:

> Upon the whole, necessity is something, that exists in the mind, not in objects; nor is it possible for us ever to form the most distant idea of it, considered as a quality in bodies.

(1978:165–6)

What Hume has in mind, in talking about the mind's spreading itself on the world, is rather what we might call (following Shoemaker 1994:295) *literal* projectivism. This is what would be involved if Basson's writers thought not merely that the note of the siren would have produced despondent feelings in human beings even if it had been heard in less dangerous times, but that the note was itself *feeling despondent*. Again, it is what would be involved if someone thought a sad song was *feeling sad*, or a wilful murder was itself *feeling a senti-*

ment of disapprobation, or a beautiful painting was itself *feeling pleasure*.

Of course, these are not intelligible thoughts, because the objects in question could not possibly possess the properties being ascribed to them. But the same is true, Hume seems to want to say, of necessity considered as a quality in bodies:

> Either we have no idea of necessity, or necessity is nothing but the determination of the thought to pass from causes to effects and from effects to causes, according to their experienced union.
>
> (1978:166)

We can think about what types of event in the world are constantly conjoined with what other types of event in the world, and we can think about what types of event in the world are constantly conjoined with what types of mental event. But there are no genuine further thoughts we can achieve by 'spreading our minds on the world'. There is only confusion.

With this perspective on Hume's account of the origin of the idea of necessary connection we can now turn to, and better understand, his explicit definitions of causation. Notoriously, Hume defines causation twice. Once as a philosophical relation:

> We may define a CAUSE to be an object precedent and contiguous to another, and where all the objects resembling the former are plac'd in like relations of precedency and contiguity to those objects that resemble the latter
>
> (1978:170)

and once as a natural relation:

> A CAUSE is an object precedent and contiguous to another, and so united with it, that the idea of the one determines the mind to form the idea of the other, and the impression of the one to form a more lively idea of the other.
>
> (1978:170)

149

It is quite clear that these two definitions are not equivalent, and that neither one implies the other, and yet Hume puts them forward as giving two views of the same object. How can this be? This is the notorious 'puzzle of two definitions' which is a hotbed of contention among commentators. The problem is not just that the two definitions assign different meanings to the term 'cause' (which might be regarded as acceptable). The problem is that they are not even *extensionally* equivalent: there are objects in the world which are causes according to the first definition but not according to the second definition, and conversely.

In order to be a cause, according to the first definition, an object has to be followed by another and all objects similar to the first be followed by objects similar to the second, and stand to them in 'like relations of precedency and contiguity'. But this could be so without anyone's observing it to be so (unless we add Berkeley's all-perceiving God to our universe). However, in that case the second definition of 'cause' will not be satisfied, for that requires that an object which is a cause be so united with a second that the idea of the one 'determines the mind' to form the idea of the other – which in the case of unobserved causes will not be so.

Again, an object can be a cause, according to the second definition, while failing to satisfy the first definition. This will be so if a constant conjunction *has been observed* between objects resembling it and a second class of resembling objects, which have also been observed to follow and to be contiguous with objects of the first class, but this observed constant conjunction does not extend beyond the sphere of observation. In this case, the psychological mechanism Hume describes will cause in us the belief that the object in question is a cause, and this belief will be true according to the second definition, but false according to the first definition.

Nevertheless, it seems clear enough what is going on, and that the problem of the inequivalent definitions poses no real problem for understanding Hume. According to Hume there are two things to be taken into account in explaining causation. There is, on the one hand, what is going on in the world, independently of its effect on any observer. And there is, on the other hand, what goes on in the mind of an observer who is prompted to apply the concept of causation to the world. As we have just seen, the case is exactly parallel, in Hume's view, to the case of moral and aesthetic properties. Here, too, there is that in the world to which we respond and there is our response, and so a similar dual definition would be possible in these cases, too. And, in fact, Hume offers precisely such a pair of definitions of virtue or personal merit in the *Enquiry Concerning the Principles of Morals*. On the one hand, he says: 'Personal Merit consists altogether in the possession of mental qualities, useful or agreeable to the person himself or to others' (1975:267); on the other hand, he asserts: 'The hypothesis we embrace is plain ... It defines virtue to be *whatever mental action or quality gives to a spectator the pleasing sentiment of approbation*' (1975:289).

Hume, as we have noted, in fact, refers to his two definitions of causation as giving 'two views of the same object' and we can understand this metaphor in the light of the foregoing. The view of the object provided by the definition of *cause* as a philosophical relation is a view of it as it is in itself, independently of its effect on any possible observer. The view of the object presented by the definition of *cause* as a natural relation is a view of it in its role as something which affects the mind in a certain way. If he had anticipated the furore his two definitions would cause among twentieth-century commentators, Hume might have expressed his second definition more carefully, giving an explicitly dispositional account (X is a cause if and only if, if X were to be observed in such and such conditions by an observer satisfying so and so constraints, the observer would judge X to be a cause), but probably he would not have bothered.

However, we can now see that there is another apparent objection to Hume's procedure which the comparison of causation with moral and aesthetic qualities only makes more obvious. This is the objection that the second definition is circular: it defines causation in terms of itself. Evidently we can, without circularity, define virtue or beauty in the way suggested above, as a disposition to *produce* certain effects in an observing mind, but applying the same procedure to causation immediately runs into trouble – for it results in a *cause* being defined as something the idea of which in a suitable mind would *cause* certain changes to take place. The only response a defender of Hume can give to this objection is to acknowledge that the second definition *would* be circular if taken by itself, but insist that it is not to be taken by itself. It is given only with the definition of 'cause' as a philosophical relation. Hence the causal verb 'determines' in the definition of 'cause' as a natural relation can be understood in terms of the definition of 'cause' as a philosophical relation, and the circularity eliminated.

Of course, this means that Hume's metaphor of 'two views of the same object' is inappropriate: the second definition can no longer be thought of as giving us a way of thinking about causation which is independent of the way of thinking of causation given us by the first definition and available to a person who is ignorant of that in the world in which causation consists. (In contrast, Hume's dispositional definition of 'virtue' provides a way of thinking of its object even to those who are ignorant of, or disagree with, Hume's thesis that it is the utility or agreeableness of a quality that produces in a spectator a sentiment of approbation.)

Given the fanfare with which Hume announced the search for the origin of the idea of necessary connection, another disadvantage of interpreting his second definition in terms of his first in this way might also seem to be that by doing so we unfortunately eliminate any trace of a reference to necessity or necessary connection in Hume's final account of causation. A possible response to this is that the verb 'determines' in the second definition can be understood as containing a reference to the impression of reflection which is produced, along with the transition from the idea of the cause to the idea of the effect, when a constant conjunction is observed. And this element of the second definition need not be deleted if the first definition is applied to eliminate the circularity.

However this may be, the most important point to note is that even if the second definition is read in such a way as to bring the idea of necessary connection into the account, it will not bring it in in the role Hume wishes, that is, as an idea of something 'the mind spreads on the world'. For if I judge something to be a cause according to the second definition, just as if I judge it to be a cause according to the first definition, I will think a thought *which could be true*. But as we have seen, if I 'spread my mind on the world' I do not think a possibly true thought. Thus no account of what there is in the world, or of the relations between the world and the mind's activities, *could* provide an account of what occurs when a judgement of causation is made, for any such an account provides the content of a thought that could be true.

There is another way in which the idea of necessary connection, thought of as something to which reference can be made in a definition of causation, is unsuited to Hume's purpose, which Stroud (1977) emphasizes.

We have seen that the impression of necessity Hume claims to find cannot be identified with the *transition* from the idea of (or impression of) the cause to the idea of (or belief in) the effect, nor can it be identified with an impression of a necessary connection which relates the idea of the cause (itself conceived as a cause) to the idea of the effect (itself conceived as an effect). It has rather to be thought of as an impression of reflection which *accompanies* the transition from the idea of the cause to the idea of the effect. But such accompaniment must be contingent. There could be creatures in whom the transition was made without any such accompaniment. Such creatures would, according to Hume's theory of ideas, lack any idea of necessity at all. But if there were such creatures they could make all the transitions in thought we do, form lively ideas (beliefs) just as we do, and in general engage in all the activities of life just as we do.

Thus it now appears that our idea of necessary connection, on Hume's account, is a redundant addition to our stock of mental ideas, something which need have no reflection in the inferences we make, the beliefs we hold and so on. Its status is that of a mere epiphenomenon, a side-product of what goes on which does not feed back into the causal stream, a wheel that can turn though nothing else turns with it (to use Wittgenstein's simile from another context). Of course, this is not what Hume intends, and his language, in which the impossible identification of the impression of necessary connection with the transition from the perception of the cause to the idea of the effect is constantly suggested, indicates his implicit awareness of the unsatisfactoriness of this position. Nevertheless, the epiphenomenal character of the idea of necessary connection is unavoidable within his theory of ideas. Just because the story Hume tells is itself *causal* through and through, and so deals in contingencies, it cannot account for our idea of causation satisfactorily if that idea is assumed to involve, as an essential element, an idea of necessary connection.

Present-day followers of Hume, however, would not take this as a criticism of their position, because, they would say, what is important in Hume is the *regularity analysis* of causation provided by the first definition. It is this which is of lasting philosophical interest, and extractable from the theory of ideas within which Hume expounds it.

It would take us too far off our track to address in detail all the criticisms of the regularity analysis in the literature on causation. But it will be worthwhile to look at the most common objection. This is that the Humean account cannot distinguish between *accidental regularities* and *law-like generalizations*. According to the Humean analysis an event X causes an event Y, if and only if X and Y stand in appropriate spatio-temporal relations (precedence and contiguity) and all events resembling X are similarly spatio-temporally related to all events resembling Y. Equivalently, we can say that X causes Y if and only if the appropriate spatio-temporal relations hold between X and Y and there are kinds A and B, to which X and Y respectively belong, such that all events of kind A are appropriately spatio-temporally related to events of kind B. In short, that X and Y are causally related if and only if the pair <X, Y> instantiates an appropriate universal generalization.

However, so understood, Hume's analysis seems open to obvious counter-examples. Suppose that whenever the factory hooters sound in Manchester the workers in Birmingham down tools and leave for home. Then (1) on a particular day the event, X, of the factory hooters sounding in Manchester, will be followed by the event, Y, of the workers downing tools and leaving for home in Birmingham, and (2) all events of the kind 'the factory hooters sounding in Manchester' will be constantly followed by events of the kind 'the workers downing tools and leaving work in Birmingham'. Assuming that the requisite spatio-temporal relation holds in this case then (which we can do, since Hume does not in the end include *spatial* contiguity in his account of causation) we are led, via the regularity analysis of causation, to the conclusion that event X is the cause of event Y. But this seems plainly incorrect (Broad 1962:455–6). The problem, of course, is that the generalization which holds in this case is plainly an accidental regularity rather than a causal law (unlike the link, by contrast, between the factory hooters sounding *in Manchester* and the workers leaving work *in Manchester*). But how is this distinction to be explained, and how (more particularly) can it be explained by a regularity theorist of causation, who follows Hume in maintaining that there are no necessary connections in the world? This, as J.L. Mackie puts it, 'is the great difficulty for any regularity theory of causation' (1974:196).

Another example to illustrate the problem comes from Thomas Reid (1941:334, cited in Fogelin 1985:168, to which the following is indebted). Night is constantly conjoined with and precedes day, but we do not wish to say that night causes day, or that a particular night causes a particular day.

There have been many attempted solutions to the general problem of distinguishing accidental generalizations from causal law. What I wish to note, however, is that these counter-examples to the regularity analysis of causation are not, in fact, counter-examples to Hume's first definition *as stated*. The point is that Hume uses the notion of *resemblance* in his first definition and this allows him, or a contemporary defender of his position, to resist the description of the putative counter-examples as ones in which a causal relation obtains. True, whenever the factory hooters sound in Manchester the workers down tools in Birmingham. But in order for the event X (the factory hooters sounding in Manchester on a particular day) to cause the event Y (the workers downing tools in Birmingham on that day), all events resembling X have got to be followed by events resembling Y. However, if we interpret 'the class of events resembling X' as referring not to the class of events consisting in factory hooters sounding in Manchester but to the wider class of events consisting in factory hooters sounding in Manchester *or* factory hooters sounding in Leeds (where the working day ends half an hour later), and interpret 'the class of events resembling Y' as referring just to the class of events consisting in workers downing tools in Birmingham, then Hume's first definition does *not* require us to think of X and Y as causally connected. Precisely because the notion of resemblance can be interpreted as narrowly or widely as we please, no possible counter-example to Hume's first definition of cause can be obtained by considering cases of this type. The same is true with respect to the day and night example, as Fogelin points out. A night is a period of darkness, a day is a period of light, so where N is a particular night and D is the following day, we can interpret 'the class of events resembling N' and 'the class of events resembling D' in such a way that it is not true that all events resembling N are immediately followed by events resembling D.

Of course, Hume's first definition of causation is invulnerable to refutation in this way only because of the lack of specificity in the notion of resemblance. But now this itself can be made an objection to Hume. For as the first definition stands it gives no guidance at all as to how widely or narrowly to interpret the notion of resemblance it involves. Since anything resembles anything in *some* respect, and nothing resembles any object other than itself in *all* respects, it allows us to regard *anything* or *nothing* as a cause.

But to see the depth of the problem Hume's use of the notion of resemblance in his first definition poses for the Humean it is necessary first to recall the role of that definition in Hume's account. As we have seen, Hume's intention is fairly evidently to specify in his first definition what is objectively there in the world, independently of observers, answering to our concept of cause. In this respect it is like his first definition of virtue as consisting in qualities useful or agreeable to the possessor of the virtue or to others, in which the effect of such a set of qualities on a spectator, the sentiment of approbation caused, is not mentioned.

However, it is very much in the spirit of Hume's philosophy to say that resemblance is *not* something that is in the world independently of observers. It is a fact that human beings are so constituted that they perceive certain things as resembling or similar, and perceive other things as dissimilar. This fact determines the concepts available to us and explains how the training in language we are exposed to results in our possession of the concepts we, in fact, have. But other creatures, without in any way being in error, could perceive quite different sets of things as resembling, and in consequence naturally acquire on the basis of their linguistic training a quite different set of concepts. Thus from a god's eye view there are no similarities in the world, or there are as many as there are possible conceptual schemes by which the world can be organized. There are, however, no 'joints' in nature such that one conceptual scheme, based on one way of perceiving similarities and dissimilarities, might cut nature at the joints and another not.

However, if this line of thought – which as I indicated seems very much in tune with Hume's philosophy, but finds its clearest expression in the present day in the work of Wittgenstein (1968) and Goodman (1955) – is accepted, then we have to say that Hume's first definition fails to isolate, as Hume wishes, the purely objective element in our notion of causation. Indeed, we must conclude that *any* attempt to define causation in terms of constant conjunction can at most provide an observer-relative notion. But, if so, the intelligibility of Hume's metaphor of the mind's spreading itself on the world once more becomes suspect. We have seen that to make sense of Hume's thought we cannot conceive of the product of such a 'spreading' as a thought about the world which could be, but in fact is not, true. But now we can see that the metaphor presupposes a distinction between the mind and the world which in the case of causation (as opposed to the cases of the aesthetic and ethical qualities which Hume wishes to view in the same way) cannot be sustained, unless resemblance is thought of as something in the world independent of human perception.

A hard question for a sympathizer with Hume must then be whether the rejection of in-the-world resemblance has not been a huge mistake. Perhaps nature does have joints, at which our conceptual schemes can, or can fail to, cut.

This is the position of at least one important contemporary philosopher whose work is otherwise very Humean in spirit – David Lewis (1983, 1984). Lewis argues that the recognition of objective resemblances in nature (or 'natural properties' as he expresses the idea) is needed in a variety of contexts: to explain the distinction between law-like and accidental generality referred to above, to explain what events are, to explain what it can mean to speak of numerically distinct things as duplicates, and (most fundamentally) to answer the scepticism about the possibility of reference implicit in Wittgenstein's discussion of rule-following. It would take us too far afield to explore these issues. I have wished only to indicate the possibility of defending Hume's first definition of cause against the criticism given and to give some sense of the depth of the issues which would have to be plumbed to assess the plausibility of the response.

Further reading

Material particularly relevant to the themes of this chapter is contained in:

Anscombe, G.E.M. (1981) *The Collected Philosophy Papers*, vol.2, *Metaphysics and the Philosophy of Mind*, Minneapolis: University of Minnesota Press.

Broad, C.D. (1962) *The Mind and Its Place in Nature*, London: Routledge & Kegan Paul.

Broughton, J. (1983) 'Causal Inferences', *Pacific Philosophical Quarterly* 64:3–18.

Cannon, R.W. (1979) 'The Naturalism of Hume Revisited', in *McGill Hume Studies*, San Diego, Austin Hill Press, pp.121–45.

Garrett, D. (1997) *Cognition and Commitment in Hume's Philosophy*, Oxford: Oxford University Press.

Goodman, N. (1955) *Fact, Fiction and Forecast*, Cambridge, MA: Harvard University Press.

Hobbes, T. (1994) *The English Works of Thomas Hobbes*, vol.1, ed. W. Molesworth, London: Routledge/Thoemmes Press.

Kripke, S. (1980) *Naming and Necessity*, revised edn, Oxford: Blackwell.

Lewis, D. (1983) 'New Work for a Theory of Universals', *Australasian Journal of Philosophy* 61:343–79.

Loeb, L. (1991) 'Stability, Justification and Hume's Propensity to Ascribe Identity to Related Objects', *Philosophical Studies* 19:237–69.

Loeb, L. (1995a) 'Hume on Stability Justification and Unphilosophical Probability', *Journal of the History of Philosophy* 33:101–31.

Loeb, L. (1995b) 'Instability and Uneasiness in Hume's Theories of Belief and Justification', *British Journal of the History of Philosophy* 3(2).

Mackie, J. (1974) *The Cement of the Universe: A Study of Causation*, Oxford: Oxford University Press.

Mackie, J. (1980) *Hume's Moral Theory*, London: Routledge.

Shoemaker, S. (1994) 'Self Knowledge and Inner Sense', *Philosophy and Phenomenological Research* 54:249–315.

Spinoza, B. (1949) *Ethics*, ed. J. Guttman, New York: Hafner Publishing Company.

Stove, D.C. (1973) *Probability and Hume's Inductive Scepticism*, Oxford: Clarendon Press.

Chapter 4

The external world

The continued and distinct existence of body

In Part IV of Book 1 of the *Treatise* Hume turns to an examination of 'the sceptical and other systems of philosophy'. As argued in the last chapter, it is in this part of the *Treatise*, rather than in the more celebrated discussions of causation and induction in Part III, that Hume's own scepticism emerges. In the first section of Part IV ('Of Scepticism with Regard to Reason'), Hume first presents what he takes to be a *sound* argument that (1) all knowledge (in the strict sense which he uses for the product of demonstrative reasoning) degenerates to probability and (2) all probability reduces to zero, so that 'all the rules of logic require a continual diminution, and at last a total extinction of belief and evidence' (1978:182). However, he argues, though if we thus follow the dictates of reason consistently all belief will be eliminated, in fact we will continue to believe. For:

> Nature, by an absolute and uncontrollable necessity has determin'd us to judge as well as to breathe and feel; nor can we any more forbear viewing certain objects in a stronger and fuller light, upon account of their customary connexion with a present impression, than we can hinder ourselves from thinking as long as we are awake or seeing the surrounding bodies, when we turn our eyes towards them in broad sunshine.

(1978:183)

The argument by which Hume thinks it can be shown that 'the rules of logic require a total extinction of belief and evidence' is generally acknowledged by commentators to be fallacious, but its main significance lies in what it shows about Hume's attitude to scepticism. Hume returns to the topic in the final section of Part IV. However, for our purposes Section 1 is of relevance for the way in which Hume thinks it leads on to Section 2 ('Of Scepticism with Regard to the Senses'), in which he turns to the topic of our belief in an external world. In both cases, Hume thinks, it is not reason which accounts for belief but human nature:

> Thus the sceptic still continues to reason and believe, even tho' he asserts that he cannot defend his reason by reason; and by the same rule he must assent to the principle concerning the existence of body, tho' he cannot pretend by any arguments of philosophy to maintain its veracity. Nature has not left this to his choice, and has doubtless esteem'd it an affair of too great importance to be trusted to our uncertain reasonings and speculations.

(1978:187)

Thus Hume's aim in his discussion is not to explore whether we are justified in our belief in an external world, or to raise the sceptical question whether an external world exists. He writes:

> we may well ask, *what causes induce us to believe in the existence of body*? But 'tis in vain to ask, *whether there be body or not*? That is a point, which we must take for granted in all our reasonings.

(1978:187)

Right at the outset of his discussion then, Hume limits his enquiry to the causes of our belief in an external world, emphasizing that this is the only question we can sensibly ask. However, this should not lead us to think that Hume's subsequent discussion will be neutral with respect to the questions of whether an external world exists or whether we are justified in believing that it does. On the contrary, the course of Hume's subsequent discussion is profoundly sceptical. He distinguishes two versions of the belief in an external world – the version of the vulgar and the version of the philosopher. He then gives an account of the belief in its vulgar form which exhibits it as *false*. But the belief in its philosophical form, Hume argues, is no better: in fact, it is merely a fallback position to which philosophers necessarily retreat when they realize that the vulgar form of the belief, which is its natural form, is untenable; it has no *primary* recommendation to reason or imagination (even the narrow imagination), but acquires all its force from the vulgar form; it is the 'monstrous offspring of two principles which are contrary to each other' (1978:215) and what is worse (as emerges finally, not in Section 2, but in Section 4, 'Of the Modern Philosophy'), it too is false, or, more carefully, can be shown to be false by an argument that 'will appear entirely conclusive to every one that comprehends it' (1978:229).

Hume begins his account of the causes of our belief in an external world, or our belief 'in body', as he puts it, by distinguishing two elements within that belief. First, there is the belief that objects *continue* to exist even when they are not 'present to the senses', and, second, there is the belief that they have an existence *distinct* from the mind and perception and are capable of existing *independently* of and *external* to us (1978:188). The first of these beliefs, Hume notes, entails the second. For, of course, what *is* so *can* be so: 'if the objects of our senses continue to exist, even when they are not perceiv'd, their existence is, of course, independent of and distinct from the perception' (1978:188). And Hume goes on to add, without explanation, that the second belief entails the first, which it does not (for what *can* be, *need not* be): 'and *vice versa*, if their existence be independent of the perception and distinct from it, they must continue to exist, even tho' they be not perceived' (1978:188). But, he says, even though 'the decision of the one question decides the other; yet that we may the more easily discover the principles of human nature, from whence the decision arises, we shall carry along with us this distinction, and shall consider, whether it be the *senses*, *reason*, or the *imagination* that produces the opinion of a *continu'd* or of a *distinct* existence' (1978:188). Of course, Hume's conclusion is that it is the third of these possible causes, imagination, which produces our belief in body, and it does so, he thinks, primarily by producing a belief in a *continued* existence.

The vulgar and philosophical forms of the belief in body

In order to understand Hume's discussion, however, it is necessary first to attend to the distinction he makes between the vulgar and philosophical forms of the belief in body. For, though Hume thinks that neither is intellectually defensible, they arise in significantly different ways and in a definite sequence, the latter only being available at all to someone who has first succumbed to the temptations of the former, but has come to see its falsehood.

To appreciate Hume's distinction it is necessary to recall that Hume *reifies* perceptions. As we know, according to Hume any mental activity involves the presence before the mind of perceptions: 'To hate, to love, to think, to feel, to see; all this is nothing but to perceive' (1978:67). And, for Hume, these perceptions are *things* to which the mind stands in the relation of *perceiving*. Moreover, there is no logical absurdity in supposing that these things, which are, in fact, perceived, might exist *unperceived*. Hume expresses this point as follows:

> what we call a *mind*, is nothing but a heap or collection of different perceptions ... Now as every perception is distinguishable from another, and may be consider'd as separately existent, it evidently follows that there is no absurdity in separating any particular perception from the mind; that is, in breaking off all its relations, with that connected mass of perceptions, which constitute a thinking being.
>
> (1978:207)

Thus, Hume insists, 'the name of *perception* renders not this separation from mind absurd and contradictory' (1978:207). That is, even though perceptions are so called because they are perceived, it does not follow that the objects so called cannot exist unperceived, just as, even though husbands are so called because they are married, it does not follow that the objects so called cannot exist in an unmarried state. (Once again, as in his discussion of a necessary connection between causes and effects, we see Hume operating with the distinction between what are called, in present-day philosophical terminology, *de dicto* and *de re* modalities, and indicating that his concern is with the latter.)

We can now explain the distinction between the vulgar and the philosophical forms of the belief in an external world. Hume thinks that, according to the vulgar, their perceptions, the things they in fact perceive, *do* continue to exist when they are not perceived. Thus they have a *continued* existence and, what follows from this, they are *distinct* from and *independent* of perception. According to the vulgar, moreover, nothing else has such a continued and distinct existence; thus perceptions comprise the furniture of the world. By contrast, according to the philosophical form of the belief in an external world (in speaking of which Hume mainly has Locke in mind) this is not so. Perceptions do not exist unperceived and so do not have a continued and distinct existence. However, there are *other* objects, distinct from perceptions, which exist when they are not perceived and, in fact, never are perceived, but cause in us the perceptions that we do perceive. These unperceived causes of perceptions, Hume thinks, must be allowed by the philosophers to be similar to perceptions: 'For as to the notion of external existence, when taken for something specifically different from our perceptions, we have already shewn its absurdity' (1978:188). In fact, he thinks, they must be allowed to be 'in their nature ... exactly the same with perceptions' (1978:218). Nevertheless, they are an *addition* to the ontology of the vulgar, a 'new set of perceptions' (1978:218) (as Hume puts it to emphasize the necessity philosophers are under to recognise their resemblance to the things we see and feel), acceptance of which is made necessary by the philosophers' denial that perceptions, properly speaking, have a continued or distinct existence. Hume thus calls this philosophical view a system of *double* existence.

Hume's aim then in Section 2 is to explain how both the vulgar and the philosophers have come to believe in the existence of an external world. He denies that the belief in either form is the product of the senses or reason and argues that the imagination is responsible for both forms of the belief, directly for the vulgar form of the belief and indirectly for the philosophical form. Thus we should look in his discussion for six components: (1) an argument that the senses cannot be the cause of the vulgar form of the belief in an external world, (2) an argument that the senses cannot be the cause of the philosophical form of the belief in an external world, (3) an argument that reason cannot be the cause of the vulgar form of the belief in an external world, (4) an argument that reason cannot be the cause of the philosophical form of the belief in the external world, (5) an explanation of the way the imagination operates *directly* to produce the vulgar form of the belief in an external world and (6) an explanation of the way the imagination operates *indirectly* to produce the philosophical form of the belief in an external world. And these six components are indeed present in his discussion, though the first four, in particular, are not always clearly distinguished.

First, then, Hume asks whether the senses can produce the belief in an external world. He dismisses, brusquely, the suggestion that the senses can give rise to a belief in a *continued* existence, for to do so they would have to 'operate, even after they have ceas'd all manner of operation' (1978:188), in order to allow one to perceive objects existing unperceived, and this, as Hume rightly says, is a contradiction.

The best the senses could do, then, would be to produce a belief in *distinct* existence. But they cannot do this either, Hume argues. For to do so they must 'present their impressions ... as images and representations' (1978:189) (if they are being thought of as producing the philosophical form of the belief in an external world), or 'as these very distinct and external existences' (if they are being thought of as producing the vulgar form of the belief in an external world).

The first possibility can be excluded, however, Hume argues. For the senses never convey anything but a single perception, and never give us the least intimation of anything beyond. When I look at a table I do not see *two* things – a perception and something it represents. Our perceptions do not present themselves to us *as* copies, even if they are. Thus the senses cannot produce the belief in a 'double existence', which must be arrived at, therefore,

> by some inference of the reason or imagination. When the mind looks farther than what immediately appears to it, its conclusions can never be put to the account of the senses; and it certainly looks farther, when from a single perception it infers a double existence, and supposes the relations of resemblance and causation betwixt them.

(1978:189)

Hume next turns to the second possibility: that the senses present our perceptions as themselves being distinct existences. This possibility is given a more extensive and complicated discussion than the first, partly because Hume distinguishes two components in the notion of a distinct existence: externality and independence. Externality is a spatial notion: X is external from Y if and only if X is located apart from Y. Independence is a modal notion: X is independent of Y if and only if X could exist even if Y did not, and X is independent of being acted on in a particular way by Y if X could exist even if it were not acted on in that way by Y.

We shall look at Hume's arguments that the senses do not and cannot produce a belief that our perceptions are themselves independent existences before looking at what he says about externality.

The first point he emphasizes in this part of his discussion is that if our senses do produce a belief that our perceptions are independent existents they operate by a 'kind of fallacy and illusion'. For, as a matter of empirically discoverable fact, our perceptions are not *independent* existences and the belief in an external world in its vulgar form is *false*. But, Hume thinks, our senses cannot deceive us in this way. To suppose that they can is to suppose that, while *none* of our perceptions has the modal property of being capable of existing independently of being perceived (a fact, however, that cannot be established a priori but only by experimental reasoning of a type Hume illustrates later in the section), some appear to us to do so and others do not appear to us to do so. However, this is not so:

every impression, external and internal, passions, affections, sensations, pains and pleasures, are originally on the same footing, and … whatever other differences we may observe among them, they appear, all of them, in their true colours, as impressions or perceptions. And, indeed, if we consider the matter aright, 'tis scarce possible it shou'd be otherwise, nor is it conceivable that our senses shou'd be more capable of deceiving us in the situation and relations, than in the nature of our impressions. For since all actions and sensations of the mind are known to us by consciousness, they must necessarily appear in every particular what they are, and be what they appear. Everything that enters the mind, being in *reality* a perception, 'tis impossible any thing shou'd to *feeling* appear different. This were to suppose, that even where we are most intimately conscious we might be mistaken.

(1978:190)

This insistence on the incorrigibility of our beliefs about what we 'are most intimately conscious' of is unsatisfying. But we have to recall the precise nature of the proposition that Hume is trying to refute: that some, though not all, of our perceptions present themselves to us as possessors of a modal property that they do not possess – being independent of our perception. Hume, in fact, is more convincing three paragraphs later, when he denies outright that this property could ever be an object of the senses, whether or not our perceptions have it. For we can perceive what things are, but not what they *are not but could be*. Knowledge of unrealized capacities can only be a product of inference:

As to the independency of our perceptions on ourselves, this can never be an object of the senses, but any opinion we form concerning it must be derived from experience and observation.

(1978:191)

Anyway, even if our senses could deceive us and even if they could present our perceptions to us as possessors of unrealized capacities that they do not, in fact, possess, we could only get from them the idea of perceptions as distinct existences if we could perceive, not only the perceptions, but also ourselves. For distinctness is a relation and to be aware of a relation we must also be aware of its relata:

> when we doubt, whether [our perceptions] present themselves as distinct objects, or as mere impressions, the difficulty is not concerning their nature, but concerning their relations and situation. Now if the senses presented our impressions as external to, and independent of ourselves, both the objects and ourselves must be obvious to our senses, otherwise they cou'd not be compar'd by these faculties. The difficulty, then, is how far we are *ourselves* the objects of our senses.
>
> (1978:189)

But, Hume argues, that we do not perceive ourselves is evident from the difficulty of the problem of personal identity. (Really, what lies behind Hume's confidence here is his yet to be explained *solution* to the problem of personal identity, which involves the contention that there is no *impression* of self at all.)

These, then, in sketchy outline, are Hume's arguments against the claim that the senses give us our belief in a world of independently existing objects. To simplify the exposition I have left out Hume's discussion of the question of *external* existence, and I must now explain why. Briefly put, the point is that externality is a spatial notion and the only intelligible sense that can be given to the claim that an object is external is that it is external to one's body. However, human bodies are *part* of the 'external world' discussed by philosophers. Hence an explanation of the belief 'in body' (that is, in an external world) in the philosophically interesting sense, cannot just take the form of an explanation of our belief in the spatial externality of objects, for that is to presuppose an already existing 'external world'. Hume makes this point himself, albeit in a somewhat unfortunate phrasing which presupposes the doctrine of 'double existence':

> properly speaking, 'tis not our body we perceive, when we regard our limbs and members, but certain impressions, which enter by the senses, so that the ascribing a real and corporeal existence to

these impressions, or to their objects, is an act of the mind as difficult to explain, as that which we examine at present.

(1978:191)

And Hume goes on to say that the real philosophical interest anyway
lies in the notion of independence rather than externality:

when we talk of real distinct existences, we have commonly more in
our eye their independency than external situation in place, and
think an object has a sufficient reality, when its Being is uninterrupted, and independent of the incessant revolutions, which we are
conscious of in ourselves.

(1978:191)

Hume sums up his discussion of the role of the senses in the following
way:

they give us no notion of continu'd existence, because they cannot
operate beyond the extent, in which they really operate. They as
little produce the opinion of a distinct existence, because they can
neither offer it to the mind as represented nor as original. To offer
it as represented, they must present both an object and an image.
To make it appear as original, they must convey a falsehood; and
this falsehood must lie in the relations and situation: In order to
which they must be able to compare the object with ourselves; and
even in that case they do not, nor is it possible they shou'd,
deceive us. We may, therefore, conclude with certainty, that the
opinion of a continu'd and of a distinct existence never arises
from the senses.

(1978:191–2)

However, he does not leave the matter there, but returns to the claim
that all our perceptions appear as they are, dependent and interrupted
beings. Earlier his emphasis was on the point that, since this is so, if
our senses were to produce a belief in the distinct existence of (some
of our) perceptions they could do so only by a sort of fallacy or illusion. Now his emphasis is different. There are, he says three classes of

impressions conveyed by the senses: those of the primary qualities, figure, bulk, motion and solidity; those of the secondary qualities, colour, smells, tastes, sounds, heat and cold; and those of the pains and pleasures arising from the application of objects to our bodies. All of these appear to our senses 'on the same footing' in the manner of their existence, that is, as dependent and interrupted, but neither the vulgar nor philosophers acknowledge this. According to the vulgar, secondary qualities are on a par with primary qualities, Hume says, as present in the objects themselves, and therefore not 'on the same footing' as pleasures and pains. Whereas, according to the philosophers, secondary qualities are on a par with pleasures and pains, as not representations of anything really present in objects, and not 'on a footing' with primary qualities. Thus neither the vulgar form of the belief in an external world nor the philosophical form can be a product of the senses, but must arise from reason or the imagination.

The claim of reason to be the origin of our belief in an external world is dealt with more briefly. Hume again distinguishes the two versions of the belief, and first considers the claim of reason to be the origin of the vulgar man's belief in an external world. He dismisses it on two grounds. First, to claim that reason is the source of the belief is to claim that it is based on *argument*, but:

whatever convincing arguments philosophers may fancy they can produce to establish the belief of objects independent of the mind, 'tis obvious these arguments are known but to very few, and that 'tis not by them, that children, peasants, and the greatest part of mankind are induc'd to attribute objects to some impressions, and deny them to others.

(1978:193)

Moreover, Hume claims, reason cannot be the source of the vulgar man's belief, because the vulgar man's belief is *false*:

For philosophy informs us, that everything, which appears to the mind, is nothing but a perception and is interrupted and dependent on the mind; whereas the vulgar confound perceptions and objects, and attribute a distinct continu'd existence to the very things they feel or see. This sentiment, then, as it is entirely unreasonable, must proceed from some other faculty than the understanding.

(1978:193)

Hume's argument against the contention that the philosopher's belief in an external world is due to reason is not given at this point, but its character is indicated:

Even after we distinguish our perceptions from our objects, 'twill appear presently, that we are still incapable of reasoning from the existence of one to that of the other.

(1978:193)

And the promised argument appears nineteen pages later, as a demonstration that 'this philosophical hypothesis has no primary recommendation … to reason':

The only existences, of which we are certain, are perceptions, which being immediately present to us by consciousness, command our strongest assent and are the first foundations of all our conclusions. The only conclusion we can draw from the existence of one thing to that of another, is by means of the relation of cause and effect, which shews, that there is a connexion betwixt them, and that the existence of one is dependent on that of the other. The idea of this relation is derived from past experience, by which we find, that two beings are constantly conjoined together, and are always present at once to the mind. But as no beings are ever present to the mind but perceptions, it follows that we may observe a conjunction or a relation of cause and effect between different perceptions, but can never observe it between perceptions and objects. 'Tis impossible, therefore, that from the existence or any of the qualities of the former, we can ever form any conclusion concerning the existence of the latter, or ever satisfy our reason in this particular.

(1978:212)

Having rejected the senses and reason as the sources of the belief in body, Hume is thus left with the imagination as the only possible source of this 'entirely unreasonable' (1978:193) belief. And since he believes that the philosophical system has no primary recommendation to the imagination his approach is first to explain how the imagination can give rise to the vulgar form of the belief. He is, therefore, faced with two tasks: to explain how the imagination can create the idea of perceptions with a 'continu'd distinct existence', and to explain how belief can reside in 'so extraordinary an opinion' (1978:195).

The causes of the vulgar form of the belief in body: constancy and coherence

Since it is the belief in body in its vulgar form with which Hume is concerned, he takes it that his task is to identify qualities of perceptions which, acting on the imagination, cause it to generate the belief that they have a 'continu'd distinct existence'. These qualities of perceptions, in concurrence with certain qualities of the imagination, will play the same role in relation to the generation of our belief in an external world that constant conjunction, in concurrence with the imagination's propensity to spread itself on external objects, plays in relation to the generation of our belief in a necessary connection between causes and effects.

The first qualities of perceptions he notices as possible causes of our belief in an external world are the involuntariness of certain perceptions and their superior force and violence. But he notices these only to dismiss them, for he points out that bodily pains and pleasures possess these qualities also, but we do not regard them as having a continued and distinct existence:

'tis evident our pains and pleasures, our passions and affections, which we suppose never to have any existence beyond our perception, operate with greater violence and are equally involuntary as the impressions of figure and extension, colour and sound, which we suppose to be permanent beings.

(1978:194)

The crucial qualities of perceptions, in the present connection, Hume claims, are rather their *constancy* and *coherence*.

In fact, these are qualities of series of perceptions, rather than of perceptions taken singly. A constant series of perceptions is just one, all of whose members are exactly alike. Thus, if I look at a mountain and then shut my eyes or turn my head, the mountain will look exactly the same when I see it again – the sequence of my perceptions of it will thus be constant, albeit gappy. Coherence is a slightly more complicated notion: a series of perceptions is coherent if it is orderly, that is, if it exhibits a pattern that other series of perceptions also exhibit. Hume writes,

> when I return to my chamber after an hour's absence, I find not my fire in the same situation in which I left it: But then I am accustomed in other instances to see a like alteration produced in a like time ... This coherence, therefore, in their changes is one of the characteristics of external objects.
>
> (1978:195)

Thus, Hume's picture is that in this case I observe a sequence of perceptions:

ABCDXXXHIJ

and on many other occasions have observed sequences of the form:

ABCDEFGHIJ

or:

ABXXXFGHIJ

and so on. The series of perceptions ABCDXXXHIJ which I receive from the fire in my study before and after my trip outside is thus a coherent series, not intrinsically, but because of its relation to the other series of this kind.

Hume spends a considerable amount of time discussing the role of coherence and elaborates its role in producing the belief in continued and distinct existence in a way that suggests it is merely an extension of our customary causal reasoning. He illustrates this with an example of a porter delivering a letter:

> I hear on a sudden a noise as of a door turning upon its hinges, and a little later see a porter who advances towards me ... I have never observ'd that this noise cou'd proceed from anything but the motion of a door; and therefore conclude, that the present phenomenon is a contradiction to all past experience, unless the door ... be still in being ... I receive a letter ... from a friend, who says he is two hundred leagues distant. 'Tis evident that I can never account for this phenomenon, conformable to my experience in other instances, without spreading out in my mind the whole sea and continent between us ... To consider these phenomena of the porter and letter in a certain light, they are contradictions to common experience, and may be regarded as objections to those maxims, which we form concerning the connexions of causes and effects. I am accustom'd to hear such a sound and see such an object in motion at the same time. I have not receiv'd in this particular instance both these perceptions. These observations are contrary, unless I suppose that the door still remains, and that it was open'd without my perceiving it.
>
> (1978:196–7)

Despite the care and attention to detail in this illustration, however, Hume does not, in fact, wish to say that 'this conclusion from the coherence of appearances' is 'of the same nature as' our reasonings concerning cause and effect. He maintains that the two are considerably different, and that the inference from coherence 'arises from the understanding and from custom in an indirect and oblique manner' (1978:197). The last phrase is an allusion to his previous discussion in Section 12 of cases of causal inference in which we are not presented with constant conjunctions but a contrariety of effects (1978:133), as when twenty ships go out to sea but I observe only nineteen to return (1978:134). Hume thinks that in such cases the belief that will be formed on the basis of past experience will be less firm and solid than that formed on the basis of an observed constant conjunction, and his chief reservation about coherence appears to be that the belief we form in an external world is *too* firm and solid to be based on the limited and contradictory evidence which he views as its basis:

> Any degree ... of regularity in our perceptions, can never be a foundation for us to infer a greater degree of regularity in some objects, which are not perceiv'd, since this supposes a contradiction, *viz.* a habit acquired by what was never present to the mind.
>
> (1978:197)

Thus, he thinks, in this case, 'the extending of custom and reasoning beyond the perceptions can never be the direct and natural effect of the constant repetition and connexion' (1978:198), but must arise from the cooperation of some other principle.

The principle he resorts to he expresses metaphorically: 'the imagination, when set into any train of thinking, is apt to continue, even when its object fails it, and like a galley put in motion by the oars, carries on its course without any new impulse' (1978:198). But, without explaining why, Hume insists that this principle is

> too weak to support alone so vast an edifice as is that of the continu'd existence of all external bodies; and that we must join the *constancy* of their appearance to the *coherence*, in order to give a satisfactory account of that opinion.
>
> (1978:198–9)

None of this is particularly convincing, however, and commentators still struggle to make sense of Hume's denial of a primary role to coherence and his insistence that in so far as it does have a role inferences from coherence are wholly unlike standard causal inferences in their nature. It is possible that Hume simply had an alternative account to offer, one that appeals to constancy, and found it more convincing.

At any rate it is now constancy that he turns to, and summarizes its role as follows (1978:199). The perception of the sun or the ocean is sometimes interrupted, but it often returns to us exactly as it was before, that is, it looks exactly the same each time I look at it. It is, therefore, natural for us to think of the interrupted perceptions not as different (which they really are), but on the contrary, to regard them as individually the same, on account of their resemblance. But we are also aware of the interruption and see that it is contrary to the 'perfect identity' of the different perceptions. The mind is thus pulled in two directions and involved in a kind of contradiction. We resolve the conflict by supposing that the interrupted perceptions are joined by a real existence of which we are insensible, that is, that they continue to exist unperceived. This supposition derives vivacity from the memory of the interrupted perceptions and the propensity which they give us to suppose them the same. Having this lively idea of their continued existence, given Hume's account of belief, *is* to believe in their continued existence. Thus the vulgar belief in an external world is explained as an erroneous product of the natural working of the imagination.

The role of identity

Having summarized in this way his account of the origin of the vulgar man's false belief, Hume turns to a more detailed analysis of the mechanism of its genesis, which he refers to as his 'system'. There are, he says, four tasks to be carried out. First, to explain the *principium individuationis*, or principle of identity. Second, to explain 'why the resemblance of our broken and interrupted perceptions induces us to attribute an identity to them' (1978:200). Third, to account for the propensity, which this illusion gives, to unite their broken appearances by a continued existence. Fourth and last, to explain the force and vivacity of conception, which arises from the propensity and constitutes belief.

Hume begins his account of identity by posing a dilemma:

the view of any one object is not sufficient to convey the idea of identity. For in that proposition *an object is the same with itself*, if the idea expressed by the word, *object*, were no ways distinguished from that [one] meant by *itself*, we really should mean nothing ... One single object conveys the idea of unity, not that of identity. On the other hand, a multiplicity of objects can never convey this idea, however resembling they may be supposed.

(1978:200)

Hume's puzzle is due to the fact that identity is a *relation*, but a relation a thing can have *only to itself*. The perception of one object, he thinks, can never give us the idea of a relation; on the other hand, the perception of more than one object can never give us the idea of a relation a thing can have only to itself. If ideas are thought of, as in Hume, as images, his puzzlement is easy to appreciate.

Thus, Hume professes himself baffled:

Since ... both number and unity are incompatible with the relation of identity, it must lie in ... neither of them. But to tell the truth, at first sight this seems utterly impossible. Betwixt unity and number there can be no medium.

(1978:200)

To solve this problem Hume has recourse to the idea of time or duration. Earlier in the *Treatise* he has argued that time implies succession – that is, change – and that the idea of time or duration is not applicable in a proper sense to unchanging objects:

the idea of duration is always derived from a succession of change-able objects, and can never be conveyed to the mind by any thing steadfast and unchangeable ... it inevitably follows ... that since the idea of duration cannot be derived from such an object, it can never, in any propriety ... be apply'd to it, nor can anything unchangeable be ever said to have duration.

(1978:37)

When we think of an unchanging object as having duration, then, this is only by a 'fiction of the imagination', by which 'the unchangeable [*sic*] object is suppos'd to participate of the changes of the co-existing objects and in particular that of our perceptions' (1978:20). The unchanging object does *not* endure, strictly speaking, but this 'fiction of the imagination almost universally takes place'; and it is by means of it, Hume thinks, that we get the idea of identity. The way this is supposed to work will be easier to comprehend if we think in terms of an example. Suppose we are gazing at the wall, on which hangs a picture of David Hume and a clock with a second hand. The picture is an unchanging object which reveals no interruption or variation and, therefore, considered in isolation, will yield the idea of unity but not that of time or duration. If the picture were *all* we were surveying and if nothing else were going on in our minds then it would be as if no time had passed. But the picture is not all we are surveying: we can also see the clock. In consequence, as well as the unchanging sequence of perceptions of the picture there is also the changing sequence of perceptions of the clock. This second sequence, which answers to our idea of number, gives us the idea of time, which genuinely applies to it. And now, Hume suggests, when we survey these two sequences together we suppose the unchanging sequence to participate in the changes of the changing sequence and thus imagine *it* to have genuine duration. Thus we arrive at the idea of identity, namely 'the invariableness and uninterruptedness of any object, thro' a suppos'd variation of time'. Here, then, Hume triumphantly concludes, 'is an idea which is a medium betwixt unity and number or more properly speaking, is either of them, according to the view in which we take it: And this idea we call that of identity' (1978:201).

Although this is hardly clear, or even coherent, one point at least emerges fairly evidently. Namely, that it cannot just be to *variable* or *interrupted* objects, in Hume's view, that the idea of identity must be inapplicable: the same must be true of invariable and uninterrupted objects. The idea of identity, to be distinct from the idea of unity, must imply duration, but duration implies change. Even the paradigm from which we get the idea of identity, then, must be a case to which it does not apply. For the notion of an object existing through a period of time without change is a contradiction in terms. If this is right the reason Hume gives for the inapplicability of the notion of identity to the perceptions in a constant series, namely their brokenness and interruptedness, is misleading or at least superfluous: given his analysis of the notion of identity there is *nothing* it is applicable to. However, the radical scepticism to which this line of thought would lead is not addressed by Hume: he is content to insist that identity is, at least, incompatible with change or interruption and with this conclusion in hand he proceeds to the next stage in the construction of his system.

His second task was to explain why the constancy of our perceptions leads us to ascribe to them a perfect numerical identity, despite their interruptedness. Hume summarizes his account of this as follows. In contemplating an identical (that is, an invariable and unchanging) object, we are doing something very different from contemplating a succession of objects related by links of resemblance, as in a constant sequence, but:

> That action of the imagination, by which we consider the uninter-rupted ... object, and that by which we reflect on the succession of related objects, are almost the same to the feeling, nor is there much more effort of thought required in the latter case than in the former. The relation facilitates the transmission of the mind from one object to another, and renders its passage as smooth as if it contemplated one continu'd object. This resemblance is the cause of the confusion and mistake, and makes us substitute the notion of identity, instead of that of related objects. However at one instant we may consider the related succession as variable or inter-rupted, we are sure the next to ascribe to it a perfect identity, and regard it as invariable and uninterrupted.
>
> (1978:253-4)

Stripped to its bare essentials the mechanism Hume refers to here is supposed to operate as follows to generate the belief that the members of a constant series of perceptions are identical. I often have impressions which seem to remain invariable and uninterrupted over a stretch of time – as when I gaze for ten minutes at a picture of David Hume. This may be depicted thus:

1   AAAAAAAAAA

I take this to be the contemplation of an identical (that is, invariable and uninterrupted) object. But if I close my eyes or look away for a few seconds I will have an interrupted sequence of perceptions:

2   AAAAXXXAAA

However, in situation (2) there is 'the same uninterrupted passage of the imagination' (1978:203) as in situation (1). Situation (2) places the mind in the same 'disposition and is considered with the same smooth and uninterrupted progress of the imagination, as attends the view of' (1978:201) situation (1). But 'whatever ideas place the mind in the same disposition, or in similar ones, are apt to be confounded' (1978:203). Thus I confound situation (2) with situation (1). But since I take situation (1) to be a view of an identical object I do the same with situation (2) and 'confound the succession with the identity' (1978:204). This is Hume's account of the second element in his system.

The third element is now easy to account for. I could regard situation (2) as a view of a single identical object, without thinking of any perceptions as having a continuous unobserved existence, if I were willing to allow that objects could have a gappy existence, that is, that one and the same object could have *two* beginnings of existence, and start up again after an interval – and this is, perhaps, not an absurd view (for example, think of clubs, which it is tempting to regard as capable of an intermittent existence, or dismantled bicycles, or Count Dracula in the Hammer horror films). But Hume insists that it is an essential part of the notion of identity that an identical object must be *uninterrupted* as well as invariable in its existence. Thus, though I cannot fail to notice the apparent interruption in situation (2), consistently with maintaining that (2) *is* a view of an identical object, I cannot allow that there really is an interruption. Consequently, I unite the 'broken appearances' by means of 'the fiction of a continu'd existence' (1978: 205). That is, I come to believe that the identical *perception A* which I earlier perceived has continued in existence while I was not perceiving it and is now again being perceived by me. I come to the *belief* that this is so, and not merely to the *thought* that it is so, because – and this is the fourth element in Hume's system – the liveliness of the memory impressions is transmitted to the thought. This, then, in Hume's view is the form that the belief in body takes in the mind of the vulgar, that is, the non-philosophers. They believe that their very perceptions have a continued and distinct existence.

The philosophical belief in double existence

Philosophers know better. Not, however, because the unperceived existence of perceptions is a contradiction. In Hume's view it isn't, as we have seen. Perceptions, like everything else, are not logically dependent on anything else for their existence – their existence in total independence of anything else is something of which we can make sense. But, *as a matter of empirically discoverable fact*, Hume thinks, perceptions are dependent and perishing existences. This, he thinks, is easily established by a few familiar experiments. 'When we press one eye with a finger, we immediately perceive all the objects to become double ... But as we do not attribute a continu'd existence to both these perceptions, and as they are both of the same nature, we clearly perceive that all our perceptions, are dependent on our organs, and the disposition of our senses and animal spirits. This experiment is confirm'd ... by an infinite number of other experiments of the same kind; from all which we learn, that our sensible perceptions are not possest of any distinct or independent existence' (1978:211).

But the psychological mechanism by which we confound situation (2) with situation (1) is too powerful even for philosophers to resist. They cannot help, any more than the vulgar, regarding situation (2) as a view of an identical object. However, they know that perceptions do not continue unperceived. To resolve their conflict all they can do is to distinguish between *objects* and *perceptions* ascribing the continuity and distinctness to the former, and the interruptedness to the latter. But such a system of 'double existence', Hume thinks, is only a 'palliative remedy' and 'contains all the difficulties of the vulgar system, with some others that are peculiar to itself' (1978:211). Thus the psychological mechanism which leads us to confound situation (2) with situation (1) necessarily involves us, whether we are philosophers or the vulgar, in intellectual error.

There are two points Hume emphasizes about this system of 'double existence' in Section 2 of Part IV. The first is that 'there are no principles either of the understanding or fancy, which lead us directly to embrace this opinion of the double existence of perceptions and objects' (1978:211). The second is that we cannot 'arrive at it but by passing thro' the common hypothesis of the identity and continuance of our interrupted perceptions' (1978:211). The first point Hume argues in two steps. First he argues that the understanding or reason can provide no possible justification for the philosophical system. We have already seen his argument for this. Since the doctrine of double existence, if true, is a contingent truth, that is, a truth about a matter of fact or existence, the only reasoning which could support it would be causal reasoning. But since, according to the system of double existence, objects, as opposed to perceptions, are never perceived, no one could ever observe a constant conjunction in which objects were causes or effects. To attempt to infer anything about objects from the patterns presented in perception would thus be like attempting to infer facts about fires from facts about smoke patterns when only smoke patterns were ever perceived.

Second, Hume argues, the doctrine of double existence could not even be a *primary* product of the imagination or fancy. Or rather, he declares himself unable to see how this could possibly be shown to be the case:

> Let it be taken for granted, that our perceptions are broken, and interrupted, and however like, are still different from each other; and let anyone upon this supposition shew why the fancy, directly and immediately, proceeds to the belief of another existence, resembling these perceptions in their nature, but yet continu'd, and uninterrupted and identical; and after he has done this to my satisfaction, I promise to renounce my present opinion.
>
> (1978:212–13)

The natural view that recommends itself to the imagination, Hume argues, is the vulgar view, even though it is provably false. Thus, he concludes, the philosophical system is necessarily a *secondary product of the imagination* – something that (1) could not be believed in on rational grounds and (2) could not be believed in at all except by someone who was at least tempted to the false view that his perceptions continued to exist unperceived.

In Section 2 this is all that Hume says about the philosophical view, but it is not all that he has to say about it because he returns to it in Section 4 ('Of the Modern Philosophy'). Here he argues, as we have seen already, that there is a necessary conflict between reason and the imagination. The philosophical view, along with the vulgar, can be seen by the application of reason to be false – though belief in an external world, in one form or other, is an unavoidable and irremovable product of the activities of the imagination.

His argument for this conclusion, briefly outlined earlier, rests on a consideration of the relation between primary and secondary qualities. Its target is the element common to the vulgar and philosophical form of the belief in an external world, that there are objects which are independent of perception, which continue to exist unperceived, and *which possess additional qualities which entitle one to think of them as material objects.* As Hume expresses its conclusion: 'it is [not] possible for us to reason justly and regularly from causes and effects [the only kind of reasoning, remember, which can assure us of any matter of fact] and at the same time believe the continu'd existence of matter' (1978:266). This conclusion is repeated in the *Enquiry*: 'the opinion of *external* existence ... [is] contrary to reason' (1975:155).

Clearly, the falsity of the belief in an external world does not follow from the fact that that belief is false in its vulgar form; nor does it follow from that fact in conjunction with the fact that it is impossible to give any reason for the belief in its philosophical form. What more is needed is an argument that the properties which we take to be definitive of material objects are none of them possessed by any independent and continuous objects, but only (if at all) by perceptions. And this, in fact, is how Hume argues. He first argues that the *secondary* qualities can be possessed only by perceptions, and next that the *primary* qualities can only be possessed by something possessing secondary qualities. Hence, he concludes, neither type of property can be possessed by something independent and continuous, and so the belief in an external world, in either its vulgar or its philosophical form, must be rejected.

The statement of this argument in the *Enquiry* makes clear the overall structure:

It is universally allowed by modern enquirers, that all the sensible qualities of objects, such as hard, soft, cold, hot, white, black, etc., are merely secondary, and exist not in the objects themselves, but are perceptions of the mind, without any external archetype or model, which they represent. If this be allowed, with regard to secondary qualities, it must also follow, with regard to the supposed primary qualities of extension and solidity; nor can the latter be any more entitled to that denomination than the former. The idea of extension is entirely acquired from the senses of sight and feeling; and if all the qualities perceived by the senses, be in the mind, not in the object, the same conclusion must reach the idea of extension, which is wholly dependent on the sensible ideas, or ideas of secondary qualities.

(1975:254)

In this passage Hume does not give any argument for the proposition that secondary properties are only in the mind; he simply asserts it as universally agreed by modern enquirers. In the *Treatise*, however, he indicates which of the arguments of the modern philosophers he finds convincing, namely 'that deriv'd from the variations of those impressions, even while the external object, to all appearance continues the same' (1978:226). And, in fact, he indicates that he finds this argument 'as satisfactory as can possibly be imagined' (1978:227).

But Hume goes beyond the modern philosophers in arguing that the same is true of primary qualities. He argues for this conclusion by arguing that only an object possessing secondary qualities can possess primary qualities, for we can form no idea of an object with primary qualities which possesses no secondary qualities. To establish this, Hume concentrates on the two primary qualities of extension and solidity. He argues that we cannot conceive of an extended object which *neither* possesses some secondary quality *nor* possesses solidity. ''Tis impossible to conceive extension, but as compos'd of parts, endow'd with colour or solidity' (1978:228). But 'colour is excluded from any real existence'. 'The reality, therefore, of our idea of extension depends upon the reality of that of solidity' (1978:228). But the idea of solidity is the idea of 'two objects, which being impelled by the utmost force, cannot penetrate each other, but still maintain a separate and distinct existence' (1978:228). Solidity, therefore, is incomprehensible alone and without the conception of some bodies which are solid and maintain this separate and distinct existence. But what idea can we have of these bodies? We cannot think of them as possessing secondary qualities, nor extension, since extension without secondary qualities presupposes solidity. Hence we cannot think of them as solid either. Thus, Hume argues, if an object lacks secondary qualities, as the modern philosophy correctly teaches is true of *all* objects except perceptions, it lacks primary qualities also. And hence 'upon the whole [we] must conclude, that after the exclusion of colours, sounds, heat and cold, from the rank of external existences, there remains nothing, which can afford us a just and consistent idea of body' (1978:229).

This argument exhibits Hume in his most sceptical mood and indeed, as we saw in the last chapter, it is at this point that Hume abandons the distinction he has insisted on hitherto between the principles of reason or the understanding and the principles of the narrow imagination. For it turns out that there are irrefutable arguments, based on principles which are 'permanent, irresistable and universal' (1978:224) and which belong to what he has previously referred to as 'reason', for the conclusion that matter does not exist; on the other hand, it is impossible to believe this conclusion, for the mechanisms of the imagination which generate the belief in an external world are equally irresistible. Thus our common belief in an external world is indubitable, but in no way justified and, being false, incapable of any justification.

Further reading

Material particularly relevant to the themes of this chapter is contained in:

Bennett, J. (1971) *Locke, Berkeley and Hume*, Oxford: Clarendon Press.

Fogelin, R. (1985) *Hume's Skepticism in the 'Treatise of Human Nature'*, London: Routledge & Kegan Paul.

Stroud, B. (1977) *Hume*, London: Routledge & Kegan Paul.

Chapter 5

The self and personal identity

The fiction of personal identity

Hume discusses personal identity in two places: in the main body of the *Treatise* in Section 6 of Part IV of Book 1 (entitled 'Of Personal Identity') and in an appendix published a year later with Book 3. In the latter he declares himself wholly dissatisfied with his treatment of the topic in the main body of the *Treatise*, but confesses that he now finds the whole matter a 'labyrinth' and that he knows neither how to correct his former opinions nor how to render them consistent: there is no discussion of the topic in the *Enquiry Concerning Human Understanding*. Unfortunately Hume fails to make clear in his recantation what he finds objectionable in his earlier account, and though commentators have produced a variety of suggestions, no consensus as to what Hume's worry was has emerged. We shall return briefly to this matter later. First we need to get clear about what the problem is that Hume is concerned with in the section 'Of Personal Identity' and what solution he there offers to that problem.

In the (recent) tradition in which Hume was writing, deriving from Locke, the problem of personal identity was seen as that of giving an account of what *constitutes* personal identity. Locke's own answer to this question has two components: a negative component and a positive component. The negative component is that personal identity is *not* constituted by identity of *substance*, whether material or immaterial, any more than is identity of 'man' (the human animal):

> It is not ... unity of substance that comprehends all sorts of identity ... but ... we must consider what idea it is applied to stand for: it being one thing to be the same substance, another the same man, and a third the same person.
>
> (*Essay* II, xxvii.7)

The positive component of Locke's answer is that what does constitute personal identity is sameness of *consciousness*:

> For since consciousness always accompanies thinking, and is that which makes everyone to be what he calls *self*, and thereby distinguishes himself from all other thinking things: in this alone consists personal identity ... And as far as this consciousness can be extended backwards to any past action or thought, so far reaches the identity of that person.
>
> (*Essay* II, xxvii.9)

Thus, Locke asserts, combining the two components of his position:

> it being the same consciousness that makes a man be himself to himself, personal identity depends on that only, whether it be annexed only to one individual substance or can be continued in a succession of several.
>
> (*Essay* II, xxvii.9)

In subsequent discussions reacting to Locke, the role of substance in the constitution of personal identity became the key issue. Butler,

Reid and Leibniz all restored, in their accounts, the link which Locke had broken between personal identity and substantial identity, the former two at the same time rejecting the centrality which Locke had given to the notion of consciousness and denying the analogy which he emphasized between personal identity and the identity of animals (see Butler 1736, Reid 1941). Leibniz attempted to develop an account of personal identity as substantial identity which retained Locke's insights by insisting that there can be no divergence between personal identity as constituted by identity of consciousness and substantial identity since identity of consciousness is itself the basis of substantial identity (Leibniz 1981).

If we read Hume as contributing to this debate on the constitution of personal identity we must understand his main contention to be an emphatic endorsement of the negative component of Locke's account: personal identity is not constituted by identity of substance. But, in fact, to read Hume in this way is to misunderstand him. For, according to Hume, personal identity is a fiction; the ascription of identity over time to persons, a mistake. It is an explicable mistake and one we all necessarily make, but nonetheless a mistake. For persons just do not endure self-identically over time. Consequently, since there is no such thing as personal identity over time, nor is there any problem of the metaphysical-cum-semantic variety presented by the question: in what does personal identity over time consist? The only problem that exists is the *genetic* one of specifying the psychological causes of the universal but mistaken belief in the existence of enduring persons, and this is the problem to which Hume addresses himself in his discussion of personal identity.

However, it is not, of course, in Hume's view (if I may so put it) a peculiarity of persons that they do not endure self-identically over time – nor does anything else which we ordinarily think of as doing so. For, as we know, Hume thinks that the idea of identity is incompatible with the idea of change: it is the idea of an object which 'remains invariable and uninterrupted thro' a suppos'd variation of time' (1978:253). Most, if not all, objects of ordinary discourse – plants, animals, artefacts and the rest – are like persons in failing to satisfy this definition, and so when we ascribe identity to them (Hume says) it is only in an 'improper sense'. Thus, for Hume, the genetic problem of accounting for our false belief in the existence of enduring persons is just a part of the wider genetic problem of accounting for our false belief in the identity over time of changing things in general. In fact, he thinks the *same* mechanism of the imagination which accounts for our ascriptions of identity over time to plants, animals and so on can equally well account for our ascriptions of identity over time to persons. This is because:

> The identity which we ascribe to the mind of man, is only a ficti-tious one and *of a like kind* with that which we ascribe to vegetable and animal bodies. It cannot, therefore, have a different origin, but must proceed from a like operation of the imagination upon like objects.
>
> (1978:253; my emphasis)

The mechanism which generates the belief in the fiction of personal identity (the identity we ascribe to 'the mind of man') is the operation by which the mind is led to ascribe an identity to *distinct perceptions*, however interrupted or variable, which Hume has earlier appealed to in his account of the genesis of our belief in an external world. He summarizes its manner of action as follows:

> In order to justify to ourselves this absurdity [that is, the ascription of identity to distinct perceptions], we often feign some new and unintelligible principle, that connects the objects together, and prevents their interruption or variation. Thus we feign the continued existence of the perceptions of our senses to remove the interruption; and run into the notion of a *soul*, and *self* and *substance*, to disguise the variation, we may farther observe, that where we do not give rise to such a fiction, our propensity to confound identity with relation is so great, that we are apt to imagine something unknown and mysterious, connecting the parts, beside their relation; and this I take to be the case with regard to the identity we ascribe to plants and vegetables. And even when this does not take place, we will feel a propensity to confound these ideas, tho' we are not fully able to satisfy ourselves in that

particular, nor find anything invariable and uninterrupted to justify our notion of identity.

(1978:254–5)

Hume indicates here how general is the application of the mechanism of the imagination by which we are led to identify distinct, but related, perceptions: it not only generates the fiction of personal identity and our belief in an external world, it also generates our belief in the identity over time of such visibly changeable things as plants and animals, and is the explanation of our regarding things (ourselves included) as substances possessing qualities, rather than as mere collections of qualities. The important point to note is that it is an essential element of this story, as Hume tells it, that the propensity we have to identify distinct perceptions is a propensity to regard them as answering to the idea of identity which he himself defines: 'an object that remains invariable and uninterrupted thro' a supposed variation of time'. If this were not our idea of identity then the psychological mechanism could not operate as he suggests. If, for instance, our idea of identity were consistent with the idea of interruption (that is, if we thought it possible that one object could have two beginnings of existence) then, as we saw in the last chapter, our propensity to identify (resembling but) temporally separated perceptions would not lead us to 'feign the continued existence of the perceptions of our senses', and thus would not lead us to our belief in an external world. Equally, if we thought of identity over time as consistent with change we would not be disposed to 'run into the notion of a *soul*, and *self* and *substance*' or be 'apt to imagine something unknown and mysterious' to *disguise* the variations. Thus, it is essential to Hume's account that our idea of identity is, in fact, the one he describes, and it is because this is so that he says:

the controversy concerning identity is not merely a dispute of words. For when we attribute identity ... to variable or interrupted objects, our mistake is not confined to the expression, but is commonly attended with a fiction, either of something invariable and uninterrupted, or of something mysterious and inexplicable, or at least with a propensity to such fictions.

(1978:225)

In denying that there is identity over time in those cases in which everyone would assert it, Hume thinks, he is not merely quibbling. For the fact is that such assertions are mistaken not just by some strict and philosophical standard with which no one but philosophers operate, but by our everyday standards for identity, and thus our everyday assertions of identity over time and through change are indicative not merely of a looseness in speech, but of actual errors in thought. Thus, according to Hume, given that our idea of identity is as he describes, we must be in error in ascribing identity over time to 'variable or inter- rupted' things – ourselves included. But given that this is *in fact* our idea of identity, plus the rest of the genetic story he tells, this error is an explicable one.

There is, however, a further point to be made, corresponding to the one noted in the previous chapter with respect to Hume's denial that interrupted but constant series of perceptions exhibit genuine iden- tity. As we observed there, given the account of the genesis of the idea of identity that Hume gives, it cannot just be to *variable* or *interrupted* objects, in his view, that identity fails to apply. The same must also be true of invariable and uninterrupted objects. The idea of identity, to be distinct from that of unity, must imply duration, but duration implies change. Thus nothing *could* answer to Hume's notion of iden- tity, not even a constant and uninterrupted series of perceptions and not even 'a *soul*, and *self* and *substance*' (1978:254).

However, just as in his discussion of the external world, so in his discussion of personal identity, Hume does not pursue the radical scepticism to which this line of thought would lead. He is content to insist that identity is, at least, incompatible with change or interrup- tion, and on the basis of this conclusion proceeds to provide his account of how our belief in an enduring self arises.

The reification of perceptions

Although Hume's insistence that our notion of identity is the one he analyses provides him with a sufficient ground for his contention that personal identity is a fiction, it is not his only ground. Another is his conception of what the nature of the self or mental subject would have to be, if it existed, and correlatively, his view of the status of perceptions.

One of the best known passages in Hume's discussion of personal identity – indeed, one of the most famous passages in any philosophical text – is Hume's denial that he is introspectively aware of any self or mental substance:

> For my part, when I enter most intimately into what I call myself, I always stumble on some particular perception or other, of heat or cold, light or shade, love or hatred, pain or pleasure. I never can catch myself at any time without a perception, and never can observe anything but the perception.
>
> (1978:252)

Many philosophers who have read this denial have found themselves in agreement. But the passage is a puzzling one. Hume writes as if it is just a matter of fact that on looking into himself he fails to find anything but perceptions, but (as many commentators have noted) this sits ill with his emphatic denial that he has any idea of a self distinct from perceptions. I can be confident that I am not observing a tea-kettle now because I know what it would be like to be doing so. But if Hume has no idea of a self he presumably has no conception of what it would be like to observe one. In that case, however, how does he know that he is not doing so? Maybe he is, but just fails to recognise the fact.

Another difficulty is that, as Chisholm puts it (1976:39), it looks very much as though the self that Hume professes to be unable to find is the one that he finds to be stumbling – stumbling on different perceptions. For Hume reports the results of his introspection in the first person: 'I never catch myself without a perception', 'I never observe anything but the perception'. Nor can he avoid doing so, if the basis of his denial is merely empirical. For suppose instead of 'I never observe anything but perceptions' he had written 'nothing but perceptions is ever observed'. Then his assertion would have committed him to denying that *anyone* ever observes anything but perceptions, and so would have gone far beyond the evidence available to him. For how could he know that? As he himself writes a little later:

If anyone upon serious and unprejudic'd reflection, thinks he has a different notion of himself, I must confess I can reason no longer with him. All I can allow him is, that he may be in the right as well as I, and that we are essentially different in that particular. He may, perhaps, perceive something simple and continu'd which he calls himself, tho' I am certain [that] there is no such principle in me.

(1978:252)

Of course, this is irony, for Hume immediately goes on: 'But setting aside some metaphysicians of this kind, I may venture to affirm of the rest of mankind, that they are nothing but a bundle or collection of different perceptions' (1978:252). But Hume is not entitled to the irony, or to any claim about the rest of mankind if, as he represents it, the basis of his report of his negative finding is empirical. For to be so entitled he needs to be able to assent not merely to the (apparently self-defeating) claim that he never finds anything but perceptions, but also to the subjectless claim that nothing but perceptions is ever found.

Hume's denial is not therefore the straightforward empirical assertion it might at first appear to be. But then what is his basis for it? Once again, we must recall that Hume reifies perceptions. Thus he starts from a conception of mental states according to which for a person to be in a mental state is for a certain relational statement to be true of that person: that he is *perceiving* a certain sort of *perception*. But if this is correct it is very natural that Hume should deny the introspective observability of the self. For if to be in any mental state is to possess a relational property of the type: perceiving a perception of type x, then no mental state can be an *intrinsic* quality of its subject. Given that the only states of which one can be introspectively aware are mental, then, introspective awareness of a self would require awareness of it without any awareness of its intrinsic qualities. But surely it makes no sense to speak of observing something introspectively if the thing has no intrinsic qualities whatsoever which one can observe by introspection. As Shoemaker (1986) puts it, this makes no more sense than it does to speak of seeing or feeling a point in empty space.

The introspective inaccessibility of the self is thus an obvious consequence of the conception of all mental states as relational which follows from Hume's reification of perceptions. And the same line of thought can be pressed further. For Hume was undoubtedly enough of a dualist to take it for granted that a mental subject would have no intrinsic qualities that were *not* mental, that is, that the physical properties of a person's body would not be intrinsic properties of a self. But, if so, it follows from the Humean conception of the mental that a self can have no intrinsic qualities at all – it must be a 'bare particular' whose only properties are relational. However, it is not hard to see how someone thinking this could conclude that no such thing could exist.

These simple reflections suffice, I think, to explain Hume's confidence in his denial of the introspective accessibility of the self. But they can be taken further if we now turn from what the Humean conception of the mental implies about the *subject* of mental states – namely that its only properties are relational ones of the type 'perceiving a perception of type X' – to what it implies about their *objects*, Hume's perceptions. What the conception implies, of course, is that these perceptions are things, indeed substances, and logically capable of existing independently of being perceived. And, as we have seen, Hume is emphatic that this is the case. Indeed, Hume thinks that *everything* which can be conceived is a substance (1978:233), since nothing is logically dependent for its existence on anything else. Everything we conceive might have been the only thing in the whole universe. This, as we have seen, is a consequence Hume explicitly draws from the conjunction of the Separability Principle and the Conceivability Principle (1978:233).

To make this consequence more vivid John Cook suggests that it follows from Hume's position:

> that there could be a scratch or a dent without there being anything scratched or dented. Indeed if we take Hume at his word, we must take him to be saying that he would see no absurdity in Alice's remark: 'Well!, I've often seen a cat without a grin, but a grin without a cat! It's the most curious thing I ever saw in all my life!'
>
> (1968:8)

Cook suggests that the flaw in Hume's reasoning that this brings out can be expressed as follows: the fact that X is distinct from Y does not entail that it is distinguishable from Y, at least not if this is to entail that 'X exists' is to be compatible with 'Y does not exist'. For the fact that X is distinct from Y does not entail that X can be identified independently of Y. Thus, the dent in my bumper is distinct from my bumper: 'the dent in my bumper' does not stand for the same object as 'my bumper'. But the dent is not distinguishable from the bumper – I could not get someone to understand which dent I was referring to without identifying the bumper in which there was a dent. Hence, Cook thinks, we can deny that Hume's argument establishes that dents are substances and by parity of reasoning we can deny that it establishes that perceptions are substances.

However, Hume has a response available. For he can insist that distinctness *does* entail independence and, by appealing to his account of 'distinctions of reason' (outlined in Chapter 2), can deny that he is committed to the absurdity that the dent might exist in the absence of the bumper. For, he can say, the dent is in fact *the very same object* as the bumper, and its distinctness is merely a distinction of reason. In fact, it is precisely to deal with such apparent counter-examples to his denial of real connections between distinct existences that Hume develops his account of distinctions of reason.

To this it can be rejoined, however, that if the appeal to the idea that the distinction in question is *merely* a distinction of reason can be allowed in this case, there is no reason not to apply it also to the distinction between the self and its perceptions, and so Hume's argument does not, after all, establish the substantiality of perceptions. Or, to put the point differently, we can allow that it follows from the conjunction of the Separability Principle and the Conceivability Principle that 'whatever can be conceived' is a substance, but then it simply becomes debatable what *can* be conceived. Not dents, if they are to be disallowed as substances; but if not, why must perceptions be admitted as conceivable?

It appears, then, that at bottom Hume's argument for the substantiality of perceptions may be question-begging. But the important point for our purposes is not what Hume's argument *does* prove, but what he thinks it proves. For if perceptions *are* thought of as substances (that is, as logically ontologically independent entities), then the self, thought of as that which has perceptions, must now appear to have a very problematic status indeed. It is implicit in this conception of the self, whether or not it is thought of as introspectively observable, that it is thought of as having a special ontological status *vis-à-vis* its perceptions and not merely as being ontologically on a par with them. And, of course, this is quite right. But it is quite right just because being in a mental state is not to be understood as bearing a special relation of 'perception' to something which has a (logically) independent existence, any more than smiling or walking is to be understood as bearing a certain special relation (of 'wearing' or 'taking') to an entity (a smile or a walk) logically capable of an independent existence. The grammar of the noun 'perception' (and that of 'idea' and 'impression') is like that of 'smile' or 'walk'. The concept of someone's having a perception is logically prior to the concept of a perception.

To put the same point in different terms, the relation between the self and its perceptions is analogous to that between the sea and its waves. The waves are modifications of the sea and perceptions are modifications of the self. But Hume, in claiming that perceptions are logically ontologically independent, denies this and thus denies the only possible basis for regarding the self, *qua* perceiver, as ontologically prior to its perceptions. That he should claim that the self is in reality nothing but a bundle of its perceptions in the section following is thus entirely intelligible. Once perceptions are reified as substances no other conception of the self makes any sense at all.

Once again, John Cook's remarks are perceptive. He points out that if the argument Hume gives were a good one then it would establish not only that perceptions are logically capable of an independent existence, but also that the same is true of qualities generally – and indeed Hume applies the argument to yield this conclusion himself (1978:222). If so, Descartes' famous analogy in the Second Meditation, in which he compares the relation between a piece of wax and its qualities to the relation between a man and his clothes, would be an appropriate one. But one consequence of this analogy is that the wax is represented as hidden beneath its garments and so as in itself unobservable. This is because the analogy implies that the assertion that the wax has any quality is in reality an assertion of a relation between it and something else. And a second consequence of the analogy is that the qualities of the wax are represented as being themselves substantial, as though they can 'stand by themselves', as a suit of armour can when no man is wearing it. But these consequences of the analogy, which is an appropriate one if the Humean argument is a good one, make it obvious that if the wax is so conceived, its existence, as anything other than that of a collection of qualities, must be regarded as highly problematic. Exactly the same is true of the self if Hume's argument is correct.

The rejection of the substantial self

With this background in mind we can now turn to the details of Hume's section on personal identity. In fact this section is continuous with the preceding one, which (though entitled 'Of the Immateriality of the Soul') contains a largely even-handed critique of both materialist and immaterialist doctrines of a substantial self, together with the striking criticism of the 'doctrine of the immateriality, simplicity and indivisibility of a thinking substance' that 'it is a true atheism, and will serve to justify all those sentiments, for which Spinoza is so universally infamous' (1978:240). The basis of this last criticism is again Hume's conception of perceptions as ontologically independent entities:

> there are two different systems of beings presented, to which I suppose myself under a necessity of assigning some substance, or ground of inhesion. I observe first the universe of objects or of body: the sun, moon, stars, the earth ... Here Spinoza ... tells me that these are only modifications; and that the subject, in which they inhere is simple, incompounded, and indivisible. After this I consider the other system of beings, viz. the universe of thought, or my impressions and ideas. There I observe *another* sun, moon and stars ... Upon my enquiring concerning these Theologians ... tell me, that these also are modifications ... of one simple substance. Immediately ... I am deafen'd with the noise of a hundred voices, that treat the first hypothesis with detestation and

scorn ... and the second with applause and veneration ... I turn my attention to these hypotheses ... and find that they have the same fault of being unintelligible ... and [are] so much alike, that ... any absurdity in one ... is ... common to both.

(1978:234; my emphasis)

Nor are matters improved for the theologians, according to Hume:

if instead of calling thought a modification of the soul, we should give it the more antient, and yet more modish name of an *action*. By an action we mean ... something which, properly speaking, is neither distinguishable, nor separable from its substance ... But nothing is gained by this change of the term modification, for that of action ... First ... the word action, according to this explication of it, can never be justly apply'd to any perception ... Our perceptions are all really different, and separable, and distinguishable from each other, and from every thing else ... [In] the second place ... may not the Atheists likewise take possession of [the word action], and affirm that plants, animals, men, etc., are nothing but particular actions of one simple ... substance? This ... I own 'tis unintelligible but ... assert ... that 'tis impossible to discover any absurdity in the supposition ... which will not be applicable to a like supposition concerning impressions and ideas.

(1978:245–6)

There could not, I think, be a clearer illustration than this of the lengths to which Hume is prepared to go in following through the consequences of his reification of perceptions – if a tree cannot be a modification of Spinoza's God, my idea of a tree cannot be a modification of me!

Turning now to the section 'Of Personal Identity', Hume proceeds very rapidly, and confidently, for reasons that I hope will now be perfectly understandable, to his conclusion that the self is nothing more than a bundle of perceptions. The whole business takes less than two pages. Some philosophers have thought that 'we are every moment intimately conscious of what we call our SELF.' But: 'Unluckily all these positive assertions are contrary to that very experience which is pleaded for them, nor have we any idea of self, after the manner it is here explained, for from what impression could this idea be derived?' Since the self is supposed to be an unchanging object any impression of self must be constantly the same throughout the whole course of our lives. But, Hume finds, looking within himself:

> There is no impression constant and invariable. Pain and pleasure, grief and joy ... succeed each other ... It cannot therefore, be from any of these impressions, or from any other that the idea of self is deriv'd; and consequently there is no such idea.
>
> (1978:251–2)

Hume goes on to raise explicitly the difficulty that his conception of perceptions as ontologically independent creates for the notion of a substantial self:

> But farther, what must become of all our particular perceptions upon this hypothesis? All these are different, and distinguishable, and separable from each other, and may be separately consider'd, and may exist separately, and have no need of any thing to support their existence. After what manner therefore do they belong to self; and how are they connected with it?
>
> (1978:252)

It is immediately after this that he issues his denial of the observability of a self distinct from perceptions, and concludes that the self can be nothing but a bundle of perceptions.

The same structure is exhibited in the 'Appendix', in which Hume summarizes his argument for the bundle theory before making his famous confession of bafflement. After arguing that we have no impression of self or substance as something simple or individual from which these ideas might be derived he goes on to spend no less than three paragraphs insisting on the ontological independence of perceptions, finally concluding that since ''tis intelligible and consistent to say that objects exist distinct and independent, without any common simple substance or subject of inhesion' (that is, it is intelligible and consistent to deny Spinoza's doctrine): 'This proposition, therefore, can never, be absurd with regard to perceptions' (1978:263–4). In the immediately following paragraph he denies the observability of the self and derives the bundle theory.

So much, then, for Hume's arguments for the bundle theory of the self. Taken together with his analysis of identity, they entitle him, he believes, to the conclusion that personal identity is a fiction, that 'the mind is a kind of theatre, where several perceptions successively make their appearance ... There is properly no simplicity in it at one time, nor identity in different' (1978:253). For the idea of identity is that of an object, that 'remains invariable and uninterrupted thro' a suppos'd variation of time'. But if the bundle theory is correct a person is nothing but a sequence of different (ontologically independent) objects existing in succession, and connected by a close relation – something like a thunderstorm. But 'as such a succession answers perfectly to our notion of diversity, it can only be by [a] mistake that we ascribe to it an identity' (1978:255).

The only question that remains then, Hume thinks, is to explain the psychological mechanism that accounts for this mistake.

Hume's account of the source of the mistake

Hume summarizes his account of this as follows. In contemplating an identical, that is, an invariable and unchanging object, we are doing something very different from contemplating a succession of objects related by links of resemblance, causation and contiguity, but:

That action of the imagination, by which we consider the uninterrupted and invariable object, and that by which we reflect on the succession of related objects, are almost the same to the feeling, nor is there much more effort of thought requir'd in the latter case than in the former. The relation facilitates the transmission of the mind from one object to another, and renders its passage as smooth as if it contemplated one continu'd object. This resemblance is the cause of the confusion and mistake, and makes us substitute the notion of identity, instead of that of related objects. However at one instant we may consider the related succession as variable or interrupted, we are sure the next to ascribe to it a perfect identity, and regard it as invariable and uninterrupted.

(1978:254)

Hume's discussion of personal identity is merely the last of several discussions in which he appeals to this mechanism. The first, in the section 'Of Scepticism with regard to the Senses', we have already encountered.

The next operation of the mechanism Hume explains is that which produces our belief (or rather the belief of the 'antient philosophers'), in substance:

> 'Tis evident, that as the ideas of the several distinct successive qualities of objects are united together by a very close relation, the mind, in looking along the succession, must be carry'd from one part of it to another by an easy transition and will no more perceive the change than if it contemplated the same unchangeable object ... The smooth and uninterrupted progress of the thought, being alike in both cases, readily deceives the mind, and makes us ascribe an identity to the changeable succession of connected qualities. But when we alter our method of considering the succession, and instead of tracing it gradually thro' the successive points of time, survey at once any two distinct periods of its duration ... the variations ... do now appear of consequence, and seem entirely to destroy the identity ... In order to reconcile which contradictions the imagination is apt to feign something unknown and invisible, which it supposes to continue the same under all variations; and this unintelligible something it calls ... *substance or original and first matter*.

(1978:220)

Once again the story is one of conflation and error produced by the faculty of 'fancy' or 'imagination'.

It is exactly the same, Hume thinks, in the case of personal identity. The same mechanism of the imagination is at work and it produces conflation and error in just the same way. The succession of my perceptions is merely a succession of distinct related objects. But because the objects in the succession are closely related the action of the imagination in surveying the succession is 'almost the same to the feeling' as the action of the imagination in considering an uninterrupted and invariable object. As in the other cases, the similarity between the two acts of mind leads me to confound the two situations and thus to regard the succession of related perceptions as really united by identity. And so I am led to believe in the unity of the self, which is as much a fiction as in the other cases of the operation of the mechanism, and 'proceed[s] entirely from the smooth and uninterrupted progress of the thought along a train of connected ideas according to the principles above explain'd' (1978:260).

All that remains to be explained, Hume thinks, is what relations do link my successive perceptions so as to bring about this uninterrupted progress of the thought. His answer is: resemblance and causation.

Our perceptions at successive times resemble each other for a variety of reasons, of course, but the one Hume stresses is that people can remember their past experience:

For what is the memory, but a faculty by which we raise up the images of past perceptions? And as an image necessarily resembles its object must not the frequent placing of these resembling perceptions in the chain of thought, convey the imagination more easily from one link to another, and make the whole like the continuance of one object?

(1978:260–1)

Given this copy theory of memory Hume is able to regard memory not merely as providing us with access to our past selves, but also as contributing to the bundles of perceptions which we can survey, elements which represent and thus resemble earlier elements; and so – since resemblance is a relation which enables the mind to slide smoothly along a succession of perceptions – as strengthening our propensity to believe in the fiction of a continuing self. In this particular case, then, Hume is able to say, with a nod of agreement to Locke, 'memory not only discovers the identity but contributes to its production' (1978:261).

But we do not remember all, or even most, of our past actions or experiences. Yet we do not affirm, because we have entirely forgotten the incidents of certain past days, that the present self is not the same person as the self of that time. Consequently there must be something else which enables us to think of our identity as extending beyond our memory. Here it would have been entirely appropriate for Hume to point out that memory is not the only source of the resemblances among our perceptions, and thus that we can imagine such resemblances extended beyond the range of our memory and by this means can comprehend ourselves as existing at times we have now forgotten. But he does not do so. Instead he appeals to causality, which has been previously introduced in his account of:

> the true idea of the human mind ... a system of different perceptions or different existences, which are linked together by the relation of cause and effect ... Our impressions give rise to their correspondent ideas: and these ideas in their turn produce other impressions. One thought chases another, and draws after it a third, by which it is expelled in its turn. In this respect I cannot compare the soul more properly to anything than to a republic or commonwealth, in which the several members are united by the reciprocal ties of government and subordination, and give rise to other persons, who propagate the same republic in the incessant changes of its parts.
>
> (1978:266)

When we think of ourselves as existing at times we cannot remember we do so, Hume says, by imagining the chain of causes and effects that we remember extending beyond our memory of them. So the causal links between our perceptions, as well as their resemblances, are crucial to our belief in a continuing self which exists at times it no longer recalls. Consequently, Hume is able to say, this time in agreement with Locke's opponents: 'In this view ... memory does not so much *produce* as *discover* personal identity, by shewing us the relation of cause and effect among our different perceptions' (1978:262).

Objections to Hume

Two objections must be noted at the outset. First, Hume is just wrong to reify perceptions or to think of them as capable of an independent existence. The comparison of the mind to a republic and of its perceptions to the citizens of the republic is thus fundamentally flawed. Second, Hume is again just wrong to think that identity must be incompatible with change. Whether this is so depends on the kind of thing to which identity is being ascribed. Some things may be by definition unchanging things. But in the case of most things this is not so. They cannot survive just any change, but what kind of changes they can survive depends on the kind of thing they are. To know what such changes are is part of knowing the definition of the kind. And persons, in particular, are entities which can survive many changes without ceasing to exist (Penelhum 1955 is the classic source of this second criticism.)

These are radical objections. If correct they show that the whole Humean enterprise is misconceived from the start. I think that they do show this. But there are other objections even if these are set aside.

One of the most obvious is the following. We not only regard ourselves as unified selves, we also have particular beliefs about which perceptions are ours. But it is not the case that all the perceptions we ascribe to ourselves are related either by resemblance or by causality. In particular, this is not true of what Hume calls 'impressions of sensation'. At present I have an impression of a desktop partly covered with sheets of writing paper. If I turn my head to the left I have an impression of a bookcase filled with books. The impression of the desktop neither resembles nor is a cause of the impression of the bookcase (nor is the desktop itself a cause of the bookcase); yet I regard both impressions as mine. Why, on Hume's story, should this be so? According to the story we are led to ascribe perceptions to a single self only when we have a propensity to identify them; and such a propensity is produced only if the action of the mind in surveying them resembles that in surveying a constant and uninterrupted object. But in the present case this will not be so. On Hume's account, therefore, I ought to have no inclination to regard both these perceptions as mine. But I do.

This criticism of Hume can be deepened by recalling his views on causality. According to these causality is not a relation we perceive between objects; rather we regard a pair of objects as related as cause and effect when we have observed a constant conjunction of similar pairs of contiguous objects and, as a consequence of this observed constant conjunction, are led to expect the second member of the pair on perceiving the first. For two of my perceptions to be related as cause and effect, then, is for them to be an instance of an observed constant conjunction between similar pairs of perceptions which has produced in me a disposition to expect the second member of such a pair whenever I perceive the first. And this is to say that for my perceptions to be causally linked in the way Hume suggests (1978:261) they would have to exhibit a multitude of long-standing constant conjunctions. But they do not do so.

Once one puts Hume's views on causality together with his account of the genesis of our belief in personal identity, therefore, it becomes evident that the latter requires the possession by the human mind of a good deal more regularity and less novelty than it actually has.

The converse objection to the one just stated is worth considering. Not only do perceptions which we self-ascribe fail to be related by resemblance or causality in the way Hume requires; these relations do obtain between perceptions which we do not self-ascribe. Many of one's perceptions are bound to resemble those of others, given that we all inhabit the same world. Presumably, also, one's perceptions, one's mental states, sometimes stand in causal connections with those of others, for instance when one talks with them. Why, then, am I not disposed to regard (some of) your perceptions as mine? Why, on the contrary, do I think of you and I as having separate minds?

Of course, Hume has an easy answer to this question. Your perceptions are not available to me as input to the mechanism which generates my belief in the unity of my mind; for I cannot 'look into your breast', as Hume puts it, and observe them. Hence the fact that they stand in relations of resemblance and causality to my perceptions and thus would be self-ascribed by me if I could observe them is neither here nor there. But this defence of Hume merely gets us to the crux of the matter. The Humean story requires that perceptions be pre-bundled, as it were, before the belief-producing mechanism he describes can operate. So Hume cannot after all reject the metaphysical-ontological question of what in fact distinguishes one mind from another and what in fact unifies the elements within a single mind. For the genetic-psychological question that he explicitly addresses presupposes that this other question is answerable. This is not to say that the metaphysical-ontological question is not answerable in Humean terms. Obviously any simple appeal to relations of resemblance and causality is bound to fail, given what we have already seen. But maybe some ingenious construction out of these relations might individuate minds in a way that fits our pre-philosophical ideas. However, Hume never addresses this question and says nothing that makes it seem at all likely that this might be so. We shall see in a moment that there is, given Hume's assumptions, strong reason for supposing that it could not be so.

The same point – that the Humean story requires that minds be 'pre-bundled' antecedently to the operation of the belief-producing mechanism Hume describes – emerges again if we look at another obvious criticism of Hume's account. This is the criticism that Hume's account of how we mistakenly come to believe in the existence of a unitary self itself presupposes the existence of unitary selves. For the story Hume tells can be true only if the mind (or the 'imagination'), as a result of surveying a certain succession of perceptions, is mistakenly led to believe in the existence of a unitary self. But if that belief is mistaken what is it that surveys the sequence of perceptions and is led into this error? Does it not seem that it must be a unitary entity of precisely the type Hume repudiates? In short, on the face of it, the explanatory story Hume tells seems internally inconsistent. What he says is that the mind, as a result of surveying a certain sort of sequence of perceptions, is caused to have a mistaken belief in the existence of a unitary self. But since 'mind' and 'self' are in this context interchangeable this seems to mean, quite absurdly, that the mind, as a result of surveying a certain sequence of perceptions, is caused to have a mistaken belief in its own existence. And, it might be added by a proponent of this criticism, perhaps Hume himself half-recognises the difficulty he faces. For it is a notable fact about the section on personal identity that, despite the fact that the primary object of Hume's account must be to explain the belief each of us has in our own identity, the perspective from which he presents the problem is determinedly third-personal. In fact, this comes out even in his manner of posing the central question of the section 'whether in pronouncing concerning the identity of a person we observe some real bond among his perceptions, or only feel one among the ideas we form of them' (1978:259).

This is the most obvious objection to Hume's discussion of personal identity. But, as Pike (1967) demonstrates, it is far from clear that it is a good one. According to Hume each mind is nothing but a bundle of perceptions. And so for a mind to perform a mental act is simply for a perception to occur in it. The mind's 'activity' consists in nothing more than perceptions occurring in it. Of course, it seems odd to say 'a bundle of perceptions confuses certain sequences of percep- tions with others' (for example), but that is merely because it is out of line with our ordinary manner of speaking. But that manner of speaking, according to Hume, embodies a falsehood.

What goes for the mind's activities also goes for its propensities or dispositions. They must be regarded as dispositions of certain bundles of perceptions to develop in certain ways over time. For example, the cash value of the claim that we are all disposed to confuse constant but interrupted series of perceptions with similar uninterrupted series is just that whenever an uninterrupted series of perceptions occurs in the particular bundle which is someone's mind, and then a similar but interrupted series occurs there, that mind or bundle will also come to contain the lively idea, or belief, that the second series is like the first. Thus, it seems, Hume's enterprise is not self-defeating in the way in which the objection under discussion envisages. For he can reinterpret talk of the mind's activities or dispositions in a way that is consistent with his belief that all that really exist are bundles of ontologically independent perceptions.

But, of course, not all bundles of perceptions will display the patterns of development which correspond, in Hume's view, to the dispositions and propensities he ascribes to minds. These patterns of development will be displayed only by certain bundles of perceptions – what we might call 'personal' bundles. But now, which are they? We have come back to the point that Hume needs an answer not only to the genetic-psychological question: 'What causes induce us to believe in unitary selves?', but also to the metaphysical-ontological question: 'What in fact unites the perceptions within a single mind and distinguishes one mind from another?' For the picture with which he operates, and with which he cannot dispense, is of perceptions objectively tied together in well-individuated bundles, prior to the operation of the belief-forming mechanism which generates, in each bundle which qualifies as a mind, a belief in its own unity.

As I said previously, Hume tells us nothing that suggests that he might be able to provide a good answer to this question. But matters are worse than that. For as Don Garrett (1981) has acutely argued, given Hume's views about causation, the relations of causation and resemblance (or any however ingenious construction therefrom) are necessarily insufficient to provide an answer to the metaphysical-ontological question, necessarily insufficient to provide an 'idea of the human mind' that corresponds to our actual idea, even after that has been purged of its vague association with metaphysical substance. Garrett argues the point thus: when we regard a pair of objects as related as cause and effect, according to Hume, all that is objectively present in the situation is precedence and contiguity in time or place. In addition there will have been an observed constant conjunction of similar pairs of objects in like relations of precedency and contiguity, as a result of which we are led, mistakenly, to regard the objects as necessarily connected. Two exactly resembling perceptions in distinct minds can differ in their causal relations, therefore, only by differing in their relations of precedence or contiguity to other perceptions. But simultaneous exactly resembling perceptions occurring in distinct minds can differ in their causal relations only by differing in their spatial locations. However, Hume is emphatic that many, in fact most, of our perceptions do not have spatial locations. This indeed is one of his main theses in the section immediately preceding his discussion of personal identity, and one of the principal components of his argument against a materialist conception of the self. He asserts:

> an object may exist and yet be nowhere, and I assert ... this is not only possible, but that the greatest part of beings do and must exist after this manner ... This is evidently the case with all our perceptions ... except those of the sight and feeling. A moral reflection

cannot be plac'd on the right or on the left hand of a passion, nor can a smell or sound be either of a circular or a square figure. These objects and perceptions, so far from requiring any particular place, are absolutely incompatible with it, and even the imagination cannot attribute it to them.

(1978:235–6)

But, of course, if there are two exactly resembling and simultaneous perceptions, X and Y, in distinct minds, neither of which is spatially located – two moral reflections or two passions, say – they cannot fail to stand to all other perceptions in exactly the same relations of resemblance and causality. If there is a bundle of perceptions containing X which qualifies as a mind in virtue of all its members being interrelated by some relation constructed out of resemblance and causality, there will be an exactly similar bundle of perceptions consisting of all the rest of the perceptions in the first bundle together with Y instead of X. And the Humean account will be quite incapable of saying why this bundle also should not qualify as a mind.

However complicated an account (in terms of resemblance and causality) Hume might give in attempting to answer the metaphysical-ontological question concerning the principle of individuation for minds, then, it must necessarily be inadequate. For any two qualitatively identical perceptions which are neither of sight nor touch and occur simultaneously will be incapable of being distinguished either by their similarity relations or by their causal relations. To be able to embrace such a 'Humean' principle of individuation for bundles one must, therefore, either abandon Hume's own most emphatically expressed view of the possibility of spatially unlocated perceptions, or reject the common-sense view that qualitatively identical perceptions may occur in two minds at the same time; in which case one can hardly claim to be giving an account of the unity of the mind in any sense that at all approximates to the one we actually have.

In presenting these criticisms of Hume's theory I have not suggested that they were the source of his subsequent dissatisfaction with his account. Whether they were, or whether it was some quite different difficulty that was worrying Hume, it is quite impossible to say. Hume is far too inexplicit. All he says is:

all my hopes vanish, when I come to explain the principles, that unite our successive perceptions in our thought or consciousness. I cannot discover any theory, which gives me satisfaction on this head ... In short, there are two principles, which I cannot render consistent; nor is it in my power to renounce either of them, viz. *that all our distinct perceptions are distinct existences, and that the mind never perceives any real connexion among distinct existences.*

(1978:635–6)

Clearly Hume no longer believes that the belief-generating mechanism he has described is sufficient to generate the belief in a unitary self. But since, as all commentators have noted, the two principles he claims that he cannot render consistent clearly are consistent, he gives no clue as to why this is so. Hume scholars will doubtless continue to speculate.

Further reading

Material particularly relevant to the themes of this chapter is contained in:

Butler, J. (1736) 'Of Personal Identity', *First Dissertation to 'The Analogy of Religion'*, repr. in A. Flew, *Body, Mind and Death*, New York: Macmillan, 1964 and J. Perry (ed.), *Personal Identity*, Berkeley and Los Angeles: University of California Press, 1975.

Chisholm, R.M. (1976) *Person and Object*, London: Allen & Unwin.

Cook, J. (1968) 'Hume's Scepticism with regard to the Senses', *American Philosophical Quarterly* 5:1–17.

Garrett, D. (1981) 'Hume's Self Doubts about Personal Identity', *Philosophical Review* 90:337–58

Locke, J. (1961) *An Essay Concerning Human Understanding*, ed. J. Yolton, London: Dent.

Penelhum, T. (1955) 'Hume on Personal Identity', *Philosophical Review* 64:571–89.

Pike, N. (1967) 'Hume's Bundle Theory of the Self: A Limited Defence', *American Philosophical Quarterly* 4:159–65.

Shoemaker, S. (1986) 'Introspection and the Self', *Midwest Studies in Philosophy* 10:101–20.

Bibliography

Anscombe, G.E.M. (1981) *The Collected Philosophy Papers*, vol.2, *Metaphysics and the Philosophy of Mind*, Minneapolis: University of Minnesota Press.

Basson, A.H. (1958) *David Hume*, Middlesex: Penguin Books.

Beauchamp, T. and Rosenberg, A. (1981) *Hume and the Problem of Causation*, Oxford: Oxford University Press.

Bennett, J. (1971) *Locke, Berkeley and Hume*, Oxford: Clarendon Press.

Berkeley, G. (1949) *The Works of George Berkeley*, vol.2, ed. A.A. Luce and T.E. Jessop, London: Thomas Nelson & Sons.

Broad, C.D. (1962) *The Mind and Its Place in Nature*, London: Routledge & Kegan Paul.

Broughton, J. (1983) 'Causal Inferences', *Pacific Philosophical Quarterly* 64:3–18.

Butler, J. (1736) 'Of Personal Identity', *First Dissertation to 'The Analogy of Religion'*, repr. in A. Flew, *Body, Mind and Death*, New York: Macmillan, 1964 and J. Perry (ed.), *Personal Identity*, Berkeley and Los Angeles: University of California Press, 1975.

Cannon, R.W. (1979) 'The Naturalism of Hume Revisited', in *McGill Hume Studies*, San Diego, Austin Hill Press, pp.121–45.

Chisholm, R.M. (1976) *Person and Object*, London: Allen & Unwin.

Cicero, M.T. (1933) *Cicero*, vol.19, trans. R.H. Rackham, Cambridge, MA: Harvard University Press, 28 vols.

Cook, J. (1968) 'Hume's Scepticism with regard to the Senses', *American Philosophical Quarterly* 5:1–17.

Descartes, R. (1984) *The Philosophical Writings of Descartes*, vol.2, ed. and trans. J. Cottingham, R. Stoothoff, and D. Murdoch, Cambridge: Cambridge University Press.

Flew, A. (1961) *Hume's Philosophy Of Belief*, London: Routledge & Kegan Paul.

Flew, A. (1986) *Hume: Philosopher of Moral Science*, Oxford: Blackwell.

Fogelin, R. (1985) *Hume's Skepticism in the 'Treatise of Human Nature'*, London: Routledge & Kegan Paul.

Fogelin, R. (1992) *Philosophical Interpretations*, Oxford: Oxford University Press.

Garrett, D. (1981) 'Hume's Self Doubts about Personal Identity', *Philosophical Review* 90:337–58.

Garrett, D. (1997) *Cognition and Commitment in Hume's Philosophy*, Oxford: Oxford University Press.

Goodman, N. (1955) *Fact, Fiction and Forecast*, Cambridge, MA: Harvard University Press.

Hobbes, T. (1994) *The English Works of Thomas Hobbes*, vol.1, ed. W. Molesworth, London: Routledge/Thoemmes Press.

Hume, D. (1874–5) *The Philosophical Works of David Hume*, ed. T.H. Green and T.H. Grose, London, 4 vols.

Hume, D. (1948) *Moral and Political Philosophy*, ed. D. Aitken, New York: Hafner Publishing Company.

Hume, D. (1975) *Enquiries Concerning Human Understanding and Concerning the Principles of Morals*, ed. L.A. Selby-Bigge and P.H. Nidditch, Oxford: Oxford University Press, 3rd edn.

Hume, D. (1978) *A Treatise of Human Nature*, ed. L.A. Selby-Bigge and P.H. Nidditch, Oxford: Oxford University Press, 2nd edn.

Hume, D. (1993a) 'A Kind of History of My Life', in D.F. Norton (ed.) *The Cambridge Companion to Hume*, Cambridge: Cambridge University Press, pp.345–50.

Hume, D. (1993b) 'My Own Life', in D.F. Norton (ed.) *The Cambridge Companion to Hume*, Cambridge: Cambridge University Press, pp.351–6.

Kant, I. (1977) *Prolegomena to Any Future Metaphysics*, Indianapolis: Hackett Publishing Company.

Kemp Smith, N. (1941) *The Philosophy of David Hume*, London: Macmillan.

Kripke S. (1980) *Naming and Necessity*, revised edn, Oxford: Blackwell.

Leibniz, G.W. (1981) *New Essays on Human Understanding*, trans. and ed. P. Remnant and J. Bennett, Cambridge: Cambridge University Press.

Lewis, D. (1983) 'New Work for a Theory of Universals', *Australasian Journal of Philosophy* 61:343–79.

Lewis, D. (1984) 'Putnam's Paradox', *Australasian Journal of Philosophy* 62:221–36.

Locke, J. (1961) *An Essay Concerning Human Understanding*, ed. J. Yolton, London: Dent.

Loeb, L. (1991) 'Stability, Justification and Hume's Propensity to Ascribe Identity to Related Objects', *Philosophical Studies* 19:237–69.

Loeb, L. (1995a) 'Hume on Stability Justification and Unphilosophical Probability', *Journal of the History of Philosophy* 33:101–31.

Loeb, L. (1995b) 'Instability and Uneasiness in Hume's Theories of Belief and Justification', *British Journal of the History of Philosophy* 3(2):301–27.

McCracken, C.J. (1983) *Malebranche and British Philosophy*, Oxford: Clarendon Press.

Mackie, J. (1974) *The Cement of the Universe: A Study of Causation*, Oxford: Oxford University Press.

Mackie, J. (1980) *Hume's Moral Theory*, London: Routledge.

Malebranche, N. (1700) *Father Malebranche: His Search after Truth, to which is Added the Treatise of Nature and Grace*, London.

Malebranche, N. (1968) *Oeuvres complètes*, ed. A. Robinet, 20 vols.

Malebranche, N. (1980) *The Search after Truth*, trans. T.M. Lennon and P.J. Olscamp, with a commentary by T.M. Lennon, Columbus: Ohio State University Press.

Mossner, C.E. (1948) 'Hume's Early Memoranda, 1729–1740: The Complete Text', *Journal of the History of Ideas* 9:492–518.

Mossner, C.E. (1954) *The Life of David Hume*, Austin: University of Texas Press.

Norton, D.F. (ed.) (1993) *The Cambridge Companion to Hume*, Cambridge: Cambridge University Press.

Parfit, D. (1986) *Reason and Persons*, Oxford: Clarendon Press.

Penelhum, T. (1955) 'Hume on Personal Identity', *Philosophical Review* 64: 571–89.

Pike, N. (1967) 'Hume's Bundle Theory of the Self: A Limited Defence', *American Philosophical Quarterly* 4:159–65.

Popkin, R.H. (1964) 'So, Hume Did Read Berkeley', *Journal of Philosophy* 61:774–5.

Pritchard, H.A. (1950) *Knowledge and Perception*, Oxford: Clarendon Press.

Reid, T. (1941) *Essays on the Intellectual Powers of Man*, ed. A.D. Woozley, London: Macmillan.

Scruton, R. (1995) *A Short History of Modern Philosophy*, London and New York: Routledge.

Sextus Empiricus (1933–49) *Outlines of Pyrrhonism*, in R.G. Bury (trans.) *Sextus Empiricus with an English Translation*, vol.1, Cambridge, MA: Harvard University Press and London: Heinemann.

Shoemaker, S. (1986) 'Introspection and the Self', *Midwest Studies in Philosophy* 10:101–20.

Shoemaker, S. (1994) 'Self Knowledge and Inner Sense', *Philosophy and Phenomenological Research* 54:249–315.

Spinoza, B. (1949) *Ethics*, ed. J. Guttman, New York: Hafner Publishing Company.

Stove, D.C. (1973) *Probability and Hume's Inductive Scepticism*, Oxford: Clarendon Press.

Stroud, B. (1977) *Hume*, London: Routledge & Kegan Paul.

Wittgenstein, L. (1968) *Philosophical Investigations*, trans. G.E.M. Anscombe, Oxford: Blackwell.

Yolton, J. (1970) *Locke and the Compass of Human Understanding*, Cambridge: Cambridge University Press.

Index